REVOLUTIONARY City©

Colonial Williamsburg

The Colonial Williamsburg Foundation
Williamsburg, Virginia

© 2009 by The Colonial Williamsburg Foundation
All rights reserved. Published 2009
20 19 18 17 16   3 4 5 6 7 8 9
Printed in China

Library of Congress Cataloging-in-Publication Data
Revolutionary city / Colonial Williamsburg Foundation.
    p. cm.
  Includes bibliographical references.
  ISBN 978-0-87935-241-7 (pbk. : alk. paper) 1. Williamsburg (Va.)—
History—18th century. 2. Historic sites—Interpretive programs—
Virginia—Williamsburg. I. Colonial Williamsburg Foundation.
  F234.W7R484 2009
  975.5'4252—dc22
                                        2009027901

Designed by Helen M. Olds

The Colonial Williamsburg Foundation
PO Box 1776
Williamsburg, VA 23187-1776
www.history.org

Image credits: p. 9, photo by Tom Green; p. 43, photo by the Colonial
Williamsburg Foundation.

Message from the Colonial Williamsburg Foundation

As the Revolution approached, Williamsburg was not only the capital of Great Britain's largest and wealthiest mainland colony in North America but also an extraordinarily dynamic community. Here were patriots and Tories, slaveholders and enslaved, dreamers and skeptics. These residents of Williamsburg struggled to resolve the contradiction between their loyalties to their mother country and families and their aspirations for freedom and independence. Some of them were bold enough to lead a revolution—political, economic, and social. Others were confused by it. Still others, loyal to the mother country, were angered and alienated. The times were tumultuous, marked by triumph and failure, promise and misgiving, excitement and sacrifice.

This book, which is based on Colonial Williamsburg's innovative and popular street theater program of the same name, tells the stories of these times. Both the program and the book span the years from 1774 to 1781. Both portray what it was like when subjects of a monarchy had the courage to turn themselves into citizens of a republic and then fought a long and debilitating war to achieve the freedom they craved.

Many of the characters in this book, such as Patrick Henry, Benedict Arnold, and George and Martha Washington, will be familiar to readers. Others, such as Barbry Hoy, the wife of a carpenter-turned-soldier, and Gowan Pamphlet, an African-American Baptist preacher, do not appear in most traditional histories. But all of these people were part of the American Revolution.

The events portrayed here were important and dramatic. But we hope *Revolutionary City* engages readers in another way as well: Today's citizens also face crucial choices that will determine the future of America and the world. Political freedom took root in Williamsburg, but it requires the continued participation of citizens today. We hope this book inspires you to play your part in this ongoing experiment in republican governance.

We are fortunate to have received generous support from longtime donors and history buffs Theresa and Michael Motes of Marietta, Georgia, who made this book possible. Mike first visited Williamsburg as a teenager, and both he and Theresa visit frequently, taking great delight in introducing their young family to all that Colonial Williamsburg has to offer. I am very grateful for the Moteses' gift to help us share more broadly the important lessons of Revolutionary City.

Colin G. Campbell
President

Credits

ADAPTED BY Philip Kopper from the scripts for Revolutionary City programming
PHOTOGRAPHY BY David M. Doody

SCRIPT CREDITS

Enemies of Government	Bill Weldon
The Gale from the North	Abigail Schumann
A House Divided	Bernie New, Melanie Collins, dramaturgical assistance by Dr. Denise Gillman
A Court of Tar and Feathers	Bill Weldon
Liberty to Slaves!	Richard Josey
The Citizen Soldier	Todd Norris
Resolved, Free and Independent States!	Bill Weldon
Lady Washington Visits the Capital	Bill Weldon
War in the West	Bill Weldon
In Desperate Circumstance	Todd Norris
The Town Is Taken	Willie Balderson
Running to Freedom	Richard Josey
The Promised Land	Bill Weldon
On to Yorktown	Ron Carnegie

ALL SCRIPTS EDITED BY Bill Weldon
ALL SCRIPTS EDITED FOR HISTORICALLY ACCURATE LANGUAGE BY Cathy Hellier
STORY LINES FOR ALL SCRIPTS DEVELOPED BY THE REVOLUTIONARY CITY SCRIPT TEAM:

Willie Balderson
Richard Josey
Todd Norris
Louella Powers
Abigail Schumann
Bill Weldon, team leader

Contents

PRELUDE 7

ACT I: COLLAPSE OF THE ROYAL GOVERNMENT, 1774–1776

    May 26, 1774: Enemies of Government 11

    April 29, 1775: The Gale from the North 17

    July 27, 1775: A House Divided 21

    September 3, 1775: A Court of Tar and Feathers 25

    November 17, 1775: Liberty to Slaves! 29

    May 15, 1776: The Citizen Soldier 33

    May 15, 1776: Resolved, Free and Independent States! 37

INTERLUDE 40

ACT II: CITIZENS AT WAR, 1776–1781

    July 25, 1776: A Declaration of Independence 45

    August 5, 1777: Lady Washington Visits the Capital 53

    June 17, 1779: War in the West 57

    September 15, 1780: In Desperate Circumstance 61

    April 20, 1781: The Town Is Taken 65

    July 4, 1781: Running to Freedom 69

    September 28, 1781: The Promised Land 73

    September 28, 1781: On to Yorktown 77

EPILOGUE 79

THE BUILDING OF REVOLUTIONARY CITY 85

SOURCES FOR REPRINTED HISTORICAL MATERIAL 90

Prelude

Boston.

Philadelphia.

And Williamsburg.

It was in Williamsburg, Virginia, perhaps more than anywhere else in America, that independence—and democracy—took root.

During the decades before the Revolution, some of Virginia's leaders protested British policies and began to articulate a new political philosophy. As early as 1765, Patrick Henry, speaking before the House of Burgesses, the elected lower house of the Virginia General Assembly, compared King George III to Julius Caesar and Charles I and suggested that the king might meet a similar end. "If this be treason," Henry is said to have exclaimed, "make the most of it."

In May 1774, the burgesses resolved that June 1, the day the British planned to close Boston's harbor in retaliation for the Boston Tea Party, would be a day of fasting, humiliation, and prayer in Virginia. Lord Dunmore, the royal governor, responded by dissolving the Assembly. The burgesses then moved to the nearby Raleigh Tavern, where they issued an appeal for a continental congress. In August, the first Virginia Convention met in Williamsburg and chose its delegates to the Congress in Philadelphia. Among them was Peyton Randolph, who was elected president of the first Continental Congress.

In April 1775, days after minutemen and militia fought British troops at Lexington and Concord, British mariners sneaked into the magazine in Williamsburg and removed fifteen half barrels of the colony's powder. Amid rising tensions, Randolph negotiated a truce. But, in June, after a second incident at the magazine, the governor fled his official residence in Williamsburg. In August, George III proclaimed the colonies to be in a state of rebellion. In November, from a ship off the Virginia coast, Dunmore issued a proclamation freeing slaves of rebels willing to join the British forces.

In May 1776, Virginia became the first colony to direct its delegates in the Congress to move for independence. The next month, the fifth Virginia Convention adopted a Declaration of Rights. This document, drafted mainly by George Mason, became a model for the Bill of Rights and, more immediately, for the Declaration of Independence that Virginia's Thomas Jefferson wrote and that the Continental Congress in Philadelphia adopted in July.

The citizens of Williamsburg suffered during the war from shortages, smallpox, and flies, among other things. In April 1781, the American traitor–turned–British general Benedict Arnold seized Williamsburg, and in June the British general Lord Cornwallis established his headquarters in the town. In

September, after Cornwallis left, George Washington and his troops arrived in Williamsburg en route to their decisive victory a few miles away at Yorktown.

The events that played out before and during the Revolution are replayed today on the streets of Colonial Williamsburg's Historic Area. That program, like this book, is titled Revolutionary City.

Act I, "Collapse of the Royal Government," covers the period between May 1774 and May 1776 as Revolutionary ideas divide loyalties, even within families. Lord Dunmore dissolves the Burgesses. Ariana and Susannah Randolph, the wife and daughter of Peyton Randolph's loyalist brother John, must cope not only with the town's gossip but also with the fact that Edmund, the family's only son, has come down on the side of the patriots. Joshua Hardcastle, another loyalist, faces the rough justice of a court of tar and feathers. Alexander Hoy, a carpenter who can find no work, argues with his wife Barbry about whether he should enlist in the army. Enslaved people consider whether to trust Dunmore's offer to free those who take up arms against their rebel masters. And representatives of free men set about establishing a new government for the independent Commonwealth of Virginia.

Act II, "Citizens at War," follows the citizens of Williamsburg through the trials they faced between July 1776 and September 1781. Just after Virginia's representatives adopted their own Declaration of Rights and state constitution, news arrives of the Declaration of Independence. Martha Washington arrives in Williamsburg to great fanfare and is confronted by a wounded soldier. Henry Hamilton, the British governor of Detroit held in the public jail, expresses his resentment at being treated as a common criminal. Barbry Hoy returns to Williamsburg to tell grim stories of the American defeats in South Carolina and her husband's uncertain fate. Benedict Arnold raises the British flag over the Capitol. As the British prepare to leave for Yorktown, enslaved people must again decide whether to trust their promises of freedom and follow them out of Williamsburg. Gowan Pamphlet, an African-American Baptist preacher, talks about his hopes for a new society. Soon after, George Washington addresses his troops as he prepares to lead them to battle . . . and victory.

ACT I

Collapse of the Royal Government
1774–1776

Enemies of Government

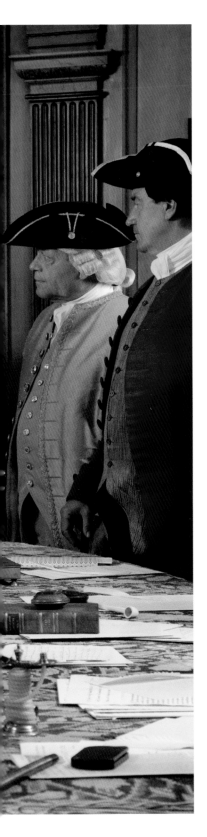

It has come to this: Lord Dunmore, royal governor of Virginia, has summoned the legislators of the colony's House of Burgesses to assemble at the Capitol. Rumor has it that he is extraordinarily angry about their resolution declaring June 1, 1774, a day of fasting, humiliation, and prayer in Virginia.

The colonies have been on edge since December 1773 when Sam Adams led a party dressed as Indians aboard a British ship and dumped its cargo— hundreds of chests of tea belonging to Britain's East India Company—into the waters of Boston Harbor. The Boston Tea Party, as it came to be called, was a response to a series of provocations dating back to 1767 when the Townshend Acts imposed duties on various goods imported from England. "No taxation without representation" was the cry of the outraged colonists. So much hostility did the Townshend Acts generate that in 1770 Parliament repealed them— except for a tax on tea, retained to remind the colonists that Britain could raise revenue in any way it pleased. The colonists responded by smuggling in Dutch tea.

The Tea Act of 1773 made matters worse. Among its provisions was one exempting the East India Company from export taxes, thus letting it undersell its competitors, even threatening to put out of business American merchants who had been selling Dutch tea smuggled into the colonies. The Tea Act pushed temperamentally conservative merchants into the patriot camp.

In response to the Tea Party, Parliament decided to close Boston Harbor until the city paid for the tea. This was the first of the Intolerable Acts that inflamed colonist tempers further. In Williamsburg, on May 24, the burgesses expressed their sympathy for Bostonians by resolving that June 1, the day the harbor was to be closed, would be a day of fasting, humiliation, and prayer throughout Virginia. The burgesses' resolution is the reason for the governor's rage, and, along Duke of Gloucester Street, the word is that he has been ranting about it all day.

Inside the Capitol, the burgesses await the governor. Here are the widely admired Speaker of the House of Burgesses Peyton Randolph and his brother John, attorney general and ever loyal to the Crown. Here are the incendiary orator Patrick Henry and like-minded Richard Henry Lee. Here are the patriotic but more cautious attorney Edmund Pendleton and colony treasurer Robert Carter Nicholas, who introduced the resolution for a day of fasting, humiliation, and prayer but fears the escalating rhetoric of rebellion. Without, townspeople gather and gossip. Among them are Jane Vobe, owner of the King's Arms Tavern; Jack Burgess, barkeep at the Raleigh Tavern; merchants and tradesmen; journeymen and freedmen; lingerers and loiterers; servants and slaves; gentle ladies followed by their maids; apprentices waiting on their masters.

The governor delivers his message to his official audience behind closed doors. Thereafter, the burgesses stream from the chambers while the crowd wonders what has happened.

Dunmore's aide-de-camp announces that the governor will address the people assembled in the yard: "Oye, Oye. His Excellency the Right Honorable John Earl of Dunmore, His Majesty's lieutenant and governor-general of the colony and dominion of Virginia and vice admiral of the same. All present attend and give ear."

The crowd quiets and looks upward as Dunmore speaks from the balcony.

"People of Williamsburg, subjects of His Most Gracious Majesty King George III," Dunmore begins, "I stand before you a vexed and troubled man. I stand before you betrayed . . . as you have been betrayed."

He recites the events of December 16 in Boston. He tells those gathered below how "traitorous men" disguised as Indians cast overboard hundreds of chests of tea and how, in order to prevent further offensive acts to private property, Parliament with His Majesty's blessing ordered Boston Harbor closed.

"The crimes of these ill-named 'Sons of Liberty' are of no importance to us here, in Virginia," the governor intones. Referring to the closing of the port, Dunmore adds, "The king's justice has been served.

"Yet, *your burgesses* disagree." Dunmore's scorn is apparent. Amid murmurs from the crowd, he continues, "Indeed, your burgesses have adopted a resolution for a day of fasting and prayer as a show of sympathy for these destroyers of property and wanton lawbreakers in Boston.

"Some may cry, 'What harm can be known by a call for prayer? What affront may be taken by recommendation for a day of fasting?' But I declare to you here today that, in one particular, such a call is not benign! It is a call for sympathy for fools and traitors! It is a most base and direct affront to His Majesty the King! Your burgesses have every awareness that days for fasting and prayer may only be decreed by His Majesty or, here in his province, by myself, his appointed executive."

These burgesses, Dunmore says, must be in "some dangerous state of delusion" to have besmirched and insulted His Most Gracious Majesty and the parliament of Great Britain.

The governor has no choice.

"This gross impertinence," he concludes, "makes it necessary for me to dissolve them, and they are dissolved accordingly. God save the king!"

"God save the king," respond those in the crowd, though with varying degrees of enthusiasm. They are quickly discussing what this means and petitioning the burgesses to explain. Adding injury to insult, if the burgesses disband without enacting required legislation, how are they to conduct necessary business—the funding of militias, the setting of rates for legal fees, the collecting of taxes? Citizens gather in small groups, questioning, arguing, until the governor descends, attended by Peyton Randolph, and struts toward his waiting carriage.

As the footman stoops to help his master into the carriage, Randolph bows and begs his ear.

"Excellency, may we express our sincerest hope that we may still be honored by your attendance, and your lady's, at the ball tonight that we have planned in celebration of her arrival in Virginia."

"Of course, Mr. Speaker, we shall be pleased to accept your hospitality. You may depend upon it." And, with that, he embarks for his residence, the so-called "Governor's Palace."

No sooner is he gone than townsfolk and proprietors descend on the Speaker and other burgesses. Jane Vobe, whose tavern must charge the rates specified by law for food, drink, and lodging, accosts Randolph.

"Will the courts remain open? There are many debts owed to my tavern. I shall not be able to collect for want of a schedule of legal fees if the court does not meet!"

"And the militia bill, Mr. Speaker," asks Jack Burgess. "How will we pay for weapons and powder? Is this the beginning of a measure to disarm us and to prevent us defending ourselves?"

On the steps of the Capitol, Patrick Henry is no longer able to contain himself.

"Friends," he addresses the crowd, "our governor has instructed that we are not to bother ourselves over the 'punishment of miscreants' in Boston. I beg leave to remind you that, upon hearing of the destruction of the tea, Lord North pronounced to Parliament that he would not hear the complaint of 'America,' not Massachusetts, but *America*, until she was at his feet."

There are some boos for Lord North from the crowd, and Henry raises his silver voice.

"And Lord Hillsborough has informed the king that he must clip the wings of some of his American turkeys in Virginia, that their high notions of freedom and liberty have caused them to roost too high in the trees. Methinks it time to inform his lordship that, if he disturbs too much his birds, he will lose their eggs for his puddings!"

The crowd laughs, but Henry's tone darkens.

"Friends, our governor has spoken of the king's justice. But, I ask you, since when is it British justice that the whole of Massachusetts is punished and all her people made to suffer because a handful of men broke the law?"

Now Richard Henry Lee addresses Randolph.

"Mr. Speaker, our countrymen understand that this attack upon Boston is an attack upon us all. If the British ships of war are able to make their way to Boston, how little time will it be before they find their way to the Chesapeake Bay? We must demonstrate that we are determined to defend our rights as freeborn Englishmen!"

To which an incredulous John Randolph retorts, "Defend our rights, Mr. Lee, in light of what, sir? The king and Parliament closed Boston Harbor in order to thwart lawlessness, restore order, and protect property. Would you have us sanction, sir, a party of criminals, who, let us remember, chose to adorn themselves as wild Indians, in a cowardly attempt to obscure their identities, so that they could anonymously break the law and wreak havoc? Is that how we are now to define patriotism, sir? A defense of lawlessness and destruction, is that now our right?"

Lee and Henry suggest protesting by stopping exports of tobacco, wheat, and lumber to Great Britain and stopping imports of all English goods.

"Gentlemen, you go too far," interrupts the attorney Edmund Pendleton.

Robert Carter Nicholas asserts that he, too, will not be a party to nonexportation and suggests that an embargo be limited to imported goods from the East India Company.

Lee and Henry will have none of this.

Peyton Randolph suggests that the members of the now dissolved House of Burgesses, the oldest representative legislature in the New World, reconvene the next day at the Raleigh Tavern to chart their course. To the relief of Nicholas and the exasperation of Henry and Lee, Randolph says a limited embargo is appropriate.

"But," he adds, "I must assert that I believe that it is now necessary, and essential, that we call for a congress of representatives from all the colonies to protect the"—and he says the next word emphatically—"*united* interests of America."

The Gale from the North

When on the morning of April 19 armed redcoats marched smartly onto Lexington Common in Massachusetts, they found the Massachusetts militia awaiting them. To the British attempt to seize the colony's stockpiles of arms and ammunition, the minutemen replied with a volley heard across these colonies before the shot thundered round the world. The American Revolution was no longer a war of words alone.

Quickly, couriers left from Boston: west via Springfield toward Albany, north via Newburyport toward Kittery, and south via Providence. Word of the fighting at Lexington and Concord took five days to reach Philadelphia, then five more to Williamsburg.

Even before the news reached Williamsburg, the capital was in an uproar over a remarkably similar incident. On April 21, a party of British seamen, acting under the orders of Lord Dunmore, crept into the magazine where the colony stored its muskets and powder. They loaded about fifteen or twenty half kegs of powder onto a horse-drawn wagon and headed out of town. Alerted, an angry crowd gathered, and only the calming influence of Peyton Randolph, Robert Carter Nicholas, and John Dixon, mayor of Williamsburg, averted violence.

It is Mann Page on horseback, galloping up and down Duke of Gloucester Street, who sounds the alarm, bringing the news from Massachusetts. At first, many assume the ruckus has to do with Williamsburg's own powder incident. Randolph, among others, fears that Page has brought news that the militias commanded by Colonel Washington and massed in Fredericksburg are marching to Williamsburg to demand that Dunmore return the gunpowder. There are mutterings in the crowd about Dunmore's theft, about it being Virginia's powder, about it being necessary to defend against the Indians.

Randolph reminds the crowd that the governor has promised to return the powder. Robert Nicholas warns that, if the colonists threaten the governor or his family, Dunmore might follow through on his threat to arm slaves and to put Williamsburg to the torch.

But Page's news is not about Fredericksburg. Near the Raleigh Tavern, he reins in his mount and shouts for all to hear:

"News from the North. Blood has been shed in Massachusetts!"

The crowd is alarmed.

"General Gage, in Boston," continues Page, "ordered troops to seize gunpowder from magazines in Lexington!"

That news rustles through the crowd, as does outrage and the suspicion that Dunmore and Gage were not acting independently.

Shouts one woman, "'Tis a conspiracy!"

Page continues, "In Lexington the citizens mustered to defend their powder and their rights. But the British troops would not hear reason! The king's troops fired upon those assembled—without provocation!"

Horrified, Randolph asks whether Page is certain. Page hands him a broadside with news carried from New England, and Randolph reads aloud:

"Watertown, Wednesday near 10 o'Clock, 15th April, 1775.

To all friends of American Liberty, be it known, that this morning, before break of day a brigade, consisting of about 1000 or 1200 men, landed at Phips's farm, at Cambridge, and marched to Lexington, where they found a company of our colony militia in arms, upon

whom they fired without any provocation, killed 6 men, and wounded 4 others. . . ."

"And now we know we're to be next!" shouts a freeholder. "Let us storm the Palace now, I say."

"Dunmore should answer for the powder," adds another.

Randolph again tries to calm the crowd. "The governor has given his assurances . . . ," he begins, only to be interrupted by voices from the crowd, which shows signs of turning into a mob.

Page now informs the crowd that six hundred militiamen are already marching from Fredericksburg . . . bound for Williamsburg.

There are boos and huzzahs from the crowd.

Randolph raises his walking stick and bellows, "Cease this now and hear me!"

So great is his authority that there is quiet. He reminds the crowd that the Virginia Convention, an extralegal, elected assembly that has begun to govern Virginia in place of the crippled Virginia General Assembly (and with many of the same members), has called upon the colonists to assume a posture of defense, and they have done so.

Randolph continues, "A posture of defense. We must not lose sight of this, gentlemen. Defense and not offense. We cannot be so eager for violence and retribution. We must seek redress. We must seek reconciliation. We must seek peace first."

Page warns Randolph of a plot that Dunmore will seize and detain delegates, including Randolph, as they travel to Philadelphia for the Continental Congress. Randolph nods soberly and then asks Page to ride back and intercept the companies from Fredericksburg.

"Tell them we have the matter in hand," he says. "Tell them to disband, to return to their homes. Williamsburg is safe."

Page rides off.

Now Randolph again addresses the crowd: "My countrymen, hear me and hear me plain. We stand at a precipice from which we dare not fall. These are dangerous times, as this most alarming news from Lexington bears witness. We must measure the consequences of all that we do. And we must act upon reason, not passion."

Randolph announces he will return to Philadelphia, under the protection of other Virginians, to the Continental Congress.

"There I will join with men from all the other colonies to attempt to find a peaceable solution to these ills that threaten to overwhelm us. Pray, give us the opportunity to reconcile with the king and avoid destruction of all we hold dear.

"My beloved Virginians," he concludes, "I ask your prayers for our success. God save Virginia!"

A House Divided

Among the fabled first families of Virginia was that of the Speaker of the House of Burgesses, Peyton Randolph, and his brother John, who counted among their cousins such other notables as Benjamin Harrison, Thomas Jefferson, and John Marshall. Their grandfather reached the Tidewater area of Virginia over one hundred years before, joined others to found the College of William and Mary, and sired a stout lineage. One son bought the house that stands today facing Market Square and sent his sons Peyton and John to London's Inns of Court where they read the common law. Returning to Virginia, Peyton was named the colony's attorney general, elected to the House of Burgesses, then chosen as its Speaker, and, on the strength of that, in May 1775, named president of the second Continental Congress in Philadelphia. His younger brother, John, succeeded him as the king's attorney and was elected to represent the College of William and Mary as its burgess. John became a favorite of the governor, and it was to John's house that Dunmore repaired on the night of June 7, amid public outrage over another incident at the magazine, this one causing minor injuries to two young men. (Dunmore sought sanctuary early the next morning aboard HMS Magdelen, *anchored in Queen's Creek.)*

Was Dunmore seeking his host's company and counsel that evening? Or the comforts of John's daughter Susannah, a comely girl whose reputation has been burned in the candle flame of the governor's affections? Susannah feels much bruised by rumors printed in the local press. As people in the colonies have become more disrespectful of the Crown and its officials, even shopkeepers dare impertinence to those among their patrons who hold Tory sentiments.

Ariana Randolph exits the Golden Ball and hails her daughter: "Susannah! I am just come from Mr. Craig's! I have here your necklace. Perfectly mended. You cannot tell where it had been broken."

Susannah's face does not warm at the return of her necklace.

"Susannah, where are your purchases? What is wrong? Are you ill, dear?"

"No, Mother, not ill but ill-used," the daughter answers, waving a copy of the *Virginia Gazette.*

Ariana reads from the newspaper an item directed at her husband: "'Your dependence on Lord Dunmore has indeed promoted your own disgrace.'

"Of course, your father is dependent upon the governor," she explains. "Lord Dunmore is the king's representative, and your father is the king's attorney. It is your father's duty to uphold the royal governor. Your father is a man of honor and supports his country, our country. You have heard such drivel before, Susannah. Think no more upon it."

Susannah is not so easily comforted.

"Yes, but now it is not solely father and his politics," she sniffs. "If you were witness to the way that woman, that shopgirl, treated me."

"Ah, my dear, I have received such treatment in the past. Have you forgotten that scathing poem that was published about me several years back in this very *Gazette*? You will recall that I kept my dignity and had the presence of mind to ignore it. And you should endeavor to do the same. You have been raised to deal with such matters with polite condescension."

"Polite? How can you remain so calm?"

"Use the paper for tinder if it will make you feel any better, dear, but behind closed doors. It is unseemly to express these unpleasant feelings in public. You are a Randolph."

"Father and Edmund are Randolphs, Mama, and their constant arguing can be heard from the street outside our home." Her mother gives her a withering look, and Susannah asks, "You wish me to follow your example?"

"Well, yes, of course."

"So I, too, should ignore the discord in our family, as you do? I should turn a deaf ear to the constant sound of argument and discord between my brother and my father? 'Tis beneath me to notice these things, as it is beneath you?"

Her mother informs her that the street is neither the time nor the place for such a discussion.

"Wait," Susannah cries. "Even our Negroes acknowledge that our household is at sixes and sevens."

Susannah turns to her lady's maid, Lucy, for confirmation. She has already complained to Lucy about the insult to her father. Ariana abruptly informs

Susannah that Lucy would not speak of such things in her presence.

"Very well, mother," Susannah says. "If we do not speak of it, then it cannot exist, can it?"

"Well then, Susannah. What is it that you wish to speak of exactly? I am all ears."

At that, the younger woman pours forth her confusion.

"Ever since I was a child, my father taught me that as English subjects we are granted rights and liberties. But Edmund speaks without ceasing of how the king has trampled upon our rights.

And it is not Edmund alone! 'Tis Cousin Jefferson . . . Cousin Cary . . . Uncle Peyton, whom you cannot deny has years of experience even beyond father's. He and all of these men oppose the views of my father."

Soothingly, Ariana assures her daughter that both her father and her uncle are looking for a peaceful resolution. But she can't help adding, "If these misguided hotheads would but listen to your father and other reasonable men, there could be harmony and concord. They would understand that the British Constitution exists to protect them. 'Tis there for the safety of Virginia—for us all. Susannah, you must realize that everything your father does is done to protect you."

"Protect me? I am the least of his concerns! Father does not consider any of us! It appears he places the king above my brother, my sister, myself, even you, mother. He is the reason I am forced to endure such insults!"

"If it is your popularity that most concerns you," her mother retorts, "you will be pleased to know that we shall soon be removing to England."

"Move to England!" Susannah cries. "For how long? Virginia is the only home I have ever known."

Now Susannah's worries turn to her brother.

"You know he will not go. Mother, he told me that he plans to join the Continental army in the field. He will not change his mind."

"I will not give up my son," says Ariana, losing her battle to fight back tears. "I cannot."

A Court of Tar and Feathers

When Lord Dunmore abandoned the Governor's Palace in Williamsburg in June, he fled to the safety of a Royal Navy ship of war. He took with him his family, his official household, and Lady Dunmore's jewelry along with the colony's civil authority—which he might as well have dropped overboard. In the absence of an established government, power came into the hands of those who took it.

The Virginia Convention, still an extralegal body but with its legitimacy enhanced by elections and the presence in its ranks of many members of the House of Burgesses, is for all intents and purposes the paramount authority governing in Virginia. The Convention has commissioned Patrick Henry as a colonel and placed him in command of two regiments of militia. Henry is a man of extraordinary oratorical gifts, but he has had virtually no experience as a military commander. The Convention has given orders that the soldiers respect the townspeople, especially women. But the soldiers, many young and away from home for the first time, are high-spirited as well as ardent and jealous in the love of liberty. They are determined to do their duty—whatever they see their duty to be and whenever an opportunity crosses their path.

Among them is Captain James Innes. As a student at the College of William and Mary, he wrote a series of articles in the Virginia Gazette *criticizing Great Britain's treatment of the colonies. Now he has organized a volunteer company partly recruited from among students at the college.*

Innes leads his patrol up Duke of Gloucester Street. He and his men are asking—nay, bullying—those they meet about whether they have seen one Joshua Hardcastle. They approach Jack Burgess, a barkeep, who tells them he is right now inside Mr. Southall's tavern, meaning the Raleigh.

"Seize him at once," Innes orders.

His men drag Hardcastle kicking and screaming out into the street, followed by other patrons of the establishment, who seem to be enjoying the spectacle.

"Are you Joshua Hardcastle?" Innes demands.

"What is the meaning of this," the man replies. "Take your hands off me! Let go of me! What do you think you're doing?"

"Are you Joshua Hardcastle, of this city of Williamsburg?"

"Yes, I am, and you have no right to handle me in this manner. I broke no law!"

Innes addresses the gathering crowd: "Gentlemen and ladies, I put it to you. The cause of America is a dire one at present. We are under attack, American blood has been spilled in Massachusetts, and, even now, General Washington is in Cambridge where he leads a patriot army against British regulars sent to our shores to enslave our countrymen. And yet there are those among us who ridicule our cause."

He turns to the prisoner, still squirming and squealing.

"Joshua Hardcastle, we, the officers and men of the companies now resident in this place, do hereby call you accountable for your actions and words. We will now call together our tribunal."

A few of his company, eager to follow what they have been told is proper protocol, agree to be Hardcastle's judges. A Captain Drew nominates Innes to preside, and the latter promptly proceeds.

"Joshua Hardcastle," Innes announces, "you are accused of, on the occasion of this evening past, in this tavern, uttering expressions highly degrading of the good men who compose the several companies now in encampment in this place. You are further accused of speaking of our American cause in a disgraceful and menacing manner. How do you plead?"

Hardcastle can only fume: "How do I plead? I do not plead at all with you. You are no authority to be pleaded to. You have no authority! I demand that you and your ruffians and bully boys unhand me and no more pester me. I will not answer to you for any utterances or expressions that I have made in regard to anything."

"Oh, you will answer," Innes warns, "and in short order. Do you wish to enter a plea?"

The defendant appeals to the crowd: "Yes, I do plead. I plead with any here who possess their sanity to assert it and assist me in being released by these lawless buckskinners who call themselves soldiers but are no more than hunting-shirted brutes that . . ."

Before he can finish, Innes orders the soldiers to gag him. Hardcastle resists, futilely. Innes then asks Drew, now acting as prosecutor, to call his witnesses. A soldier from their company is sworn in, and he recounts how he saw Hardcastle last night at the Raleigh Tavern.

"He was sayin' many things of a very insultin' nature regardin' the men in the camp . . . that we was so poor at drill that he thought people should pray for us that we not shoot ourselves or run each other through with our own bayonets."

There are angry shouts from the soldiers and a groan from Hardcastle.

The soldier continues, "He called us Henry's toy soldiers and said that, poor as we was at soldierin' and with Patrick Henry as our commander, that the British would mow through us easier than cuttin' ripe wheat on a cool day. He said he would take great delight in watchin' it occur."

The next witness, barkeep Jack Burgess, confirms what Hardcastle said, adding that he has been saying such things for months.

"After we heard that Mr. Henry said 'Give me liberty or give me death,' Hardcastle said he didn't deserve the one so he hoped the patriot would soon be accommodated in his other desire. When the Congress met again in Philadelphia, he said the best thing to happen would be for some loyal subject of the king to set a torch to Carpenter's Hall."

The crowd is at this point nearing a frenzy, but Innes takes the gag off and allows Hardcastle his say. Frightened but defiant, Hardcastle does not deny what he said, but he insists that he did not mean any real harm should come to those men.

"I have a right as a British subject to speak my mind," he declares. "Not just a right but a duty to speak against the treason now being committed . . ."

Innes has heard enough. He quickly polls the "jurors" and equally quickly declares the accused guilty as charged. Drew suggests a number of options as punishments: Hardcastle could show remorse and make apologies, he could be marched through the street at a slow drumbeat and subjected to whatever physical abuse or insults any would inflict upon him, or he could be tarred and feathered.

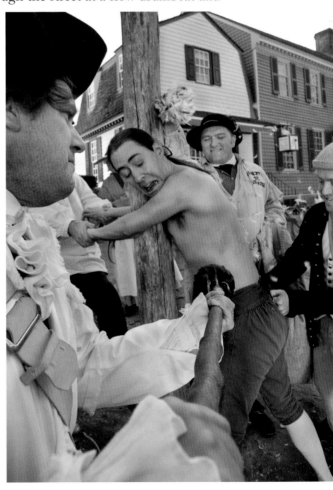

Drew describes the procedure to the enthusiastic crowd: "We apply a coat of tar and feathers and ride him through town on a fence rail to be scorned and ridiculed."

The crowd, led by Innes, enthusiastically endorses this option. The soldiers drag Hardcastle to the liberty pole across the street, set up for just this purpose. They strip off his coat, waistcoat, and shirt. Innes dips a mop into the kettle of tar and prepares to apply it to Hardcastle's back.

Faced with the prospect of not just humiliation but pain and maiming, Hardcastle cries out, "Stop! Stop! I will apologize. I beg you, stop!"

Some in the crowd are clearly disappointed. But Innes extracts a promise that Hardcastle will never again be guilty of a like offense and that his apology will be published in the *Virginia Gazette*s. The soldiers escort him into the tavern to sign his apology.

"Our business is done," declares Innes, "but all here should be very certain of this as a warning to those who may hereafter sport with our great and glorious cause. God save America!"

Liberty to Slaves!

After fleeing Williamsburg, Lord Dunmore could no longer dictate what went on in Virginia, but he could still create havoc throughout the colony. From his headquarters on a Royal Navy ship, Dunmore ordered lethal raids such as one on November 15 at Kemp's Landing in Princess Anne County near Norfolk. The poorly trained local militia tried to ambush the British but ended up fleeing in panic.

Emboldened by his victory, Dunmore issued a proclamation that "all indented servants, negroes, or others (appertaining to rebels) free, that are able and willing to bear arms" for the king. In doing so, Dunmore made real the greatest fear of many colonists: he freed their slaves.

Word of his emancipation proclamation spread quickly, and slave owners were indeed greatly incensed. But Dunmore misjudged the reaction of moderate whites. Many saw the proclamation as a far more radical act than anything the patriots had proposed, and many who had wavered now embraced the rebel cause.

And what of the enslaved Americans themselves? Dunmore's proclamation divided black families as well as white. Many saw the chance for freedom and joined the British, though the actual number is disputed. Many others supported the patriot cause. They may have feared that Dunmore would not keep his word or that they would be captured and returned to their masters, or they may have hoped that the liberty of which colonists spoke might someday apply to them.

Let's listen in on one such discussion. Among those pondering their choices are Kate, a slave at the Raleigh Tavern; Eve, a maid in Peyton Randolph's household; William Wells from nearby Mulberry Island; and Edith Cumbo, a free black working as a laundress. As they speak, they are always on the lookout for constables or slave patrols, for a meeting like this is forbidden.

It is Eve who arrives with a copy of the proclamation and hands it to Kate.

"Best be careful with that," Eve warns. "Some might call this sedition. Change for the Negro . . . change for us all."

Eve looks around nervously.

"I've stayed long enough. Good day to you all. God save the king!"

The others are impatient to know what's going on, and Kate explains: "This here a proclamation. Lord Dunmore has declared martial law!"

"So the gentlemen ain't the law no more," says William. "Soldiers is

the law. But what that got to do with us?"

Kate answers, "This here is a freedom paper for every Negro and indentured servant in this colony. I wouldn't be surprised if Negroes from Maryland and the Carolinas were making their way to Norfolk."

"I knew it!" William exults. "I told you that the British'd give us freedom. If being free mean getting to Norfolk, we can get there."

"And what if we get caught?" asks Kate. "They'll kill us dead for sure. I know folks that hanged for less than this."

"Perhaps you're right," answers Edith. "But what if you don't go? And pass on this chance for freedom? You might as well consider yourself dead then."

"William, do you really think that His Lordship will keep his promise?" ponders Kate. She is also worried about whether the governor is taking women as well as men.

"In truth, I don't know," he answers. "I just know we ought to do something."

He takes the proclamation and starts to read it to himself.

"I suppose there's so much to being free," muses Kate. "I've thought on it before but never thought it would happen. I just want to be with my children and not worry 'bout no man taking 'em from me."

William suddenly looks dejected.

"Oh, Lord," he moans.

Kate wants to know what's wrong. He points to the paper.

"You know I can't read it," she says. "Just tell me what it say."

He reads, "'And I do hereby farther declare all indented servants, negroes, or others (appertaining to rebels) free, that are able and willing to bear arms . . .'"

"Well, what's wrong?" Kate asks.

Edith explains: "Lord Dunmore is calling for all indentured servants and slaves who are owned by *rebel* masters, those who are against the British. Kate, William's master ain't a rebel. He's loyal to the British."

Kate looks at William.

"I'm so sorry. I didn't know." Her voice trails off.

"After all that waiting, all that praying," he says. "All for naught."

William crumples the paper, puts his Bible down on the bench, and walks away. Kate starts to rush after him, but Edith stops her and tells her to take him his Bible.

"He'll need this more now than ever," she says.

May 15, 1776

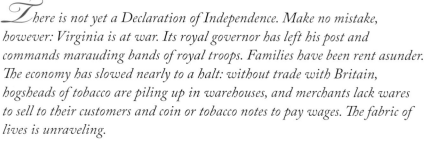

The Citizen Soldier

There is not yet a Declaration of Independence. Make no mistake, however: Virginia is at war. Its royal governor has left his post and commands marauding bands of royal troops. Families have been rent asunder. The economy has slowed nearly to a halt: without trade with Britain, hogsheads of tobacco are piling up in warehouses, and merchants lack wares to sell to their customers and coin or tobacco notes to pay wages. The fabric of lives is unraveling.

Alexander Hoy, a carpenter, and his wife, Barbry, are two such lives. An upright man known as a good worker, Alexander has lost the wherewithal to pay his debts, even to purchase salt, a necessity for preserving food. He and Barbry, along with their aged horse, have come to town to find whatever work they can.

No sooner do they turn onto Duke of Gloucester Street than a creditor shouts from a window, "Hey there, Hoy, have you the five pounds you owe me?"

Others call out similar demands. To some, he stammers an apology; to others, he is too ashamed to reply. Alexander leaves the horse with Barbry and goes to meet with James Southall, owner of the Raleigh Tavern, in the hope that he can offer help. He cannot.

"I am sorry, Hoy," he explains. "Everyone is indebted now. I am extended myself and I cannot extend further. I know you to be a fair workman. I am sorry. Return to me in a month. Give me one month."

"And what shall I feed my children for a month?" Hoy asks Southall . . . and himself.

He asks a passing gentleman, "Do you have work for a carpenter, sir, paying work?"

But the gentleman turns his head and hurries on.

"Madam, need you a chest or a table?"

Again, no.

Despairing, Hoy asks no one in particular, "Pray, how about a coffin? What say you? Coffins for the whole family. One for each. Coffins for the dying soldiers? I could build all of us coffins!"

Barbry, powerless and afraid, stands frozen amid the commotion. Captain James Innes has also been standing and watching. Now he approaches Alexander.

"You could enlist," he suggests.

Alexander looks at him, and Innes continues.

"You could enlist in the army. You could be in George Washington's army, Hoy. That's how you could provide. You could help the fight."

Dully, Hoy asks, "Enlist?"

Now Innes addresses Barbry.

"He could enlist, madam, enlist in the Continental army. You'd get ten pounds and a land bounty if your husband enlisted."

"Mr. Hoy is a carpenter, sir, not a soldier."

But Alexander is paying attention. He cannot remember the last time he earned ten pounds. He reminds his wife that it could pay their rent.

"No, Mr. Hoy!" Barbry cries. "I'll not be giving you to the army. We cannot be living out there, far from everything, without you." She adds that the ten pounds is paper money, and she well knows how little that's worth.

Alexander can see no other choice but to enlist, and Innes drives home his point by suggesting an even more disheartening option.

"I've seen your family. Your daughter looks to be strong. There are genteel families who would take care of her, let her earn her way."

"You're asking my wife to give away her oldest?" answers Alexander. "My Mary, to be a servant, a slave almost?"

"I will not be giving my Mary to no one," says Barbry.

And that leaves Alexander Hoy with only the one choice.

"Barbry, a man is got to provide some for his family. Some say it be over in a year. You have the farm, and our man, Henry . . ."

"Henry? Henry's the oldest slave in the county! He eats more than he ever works.

We need you, Alexander! What if you get killed?"

"Then you are better off."

She pleads, she objects, but he has made up his mind.

"They give you a pension then."

Gently, Innes tells Barbry that her husband will be serving his country, fighting for freedom.

"Mrs. Hoy," her husband tells her, "you ought to be going now and get home to those girls 'fore it gets too dark."

They cling to each, and he tries to reassure her.

"I am a good carpenter. Maybe they'll have me do work like fixing wagons and carts and such. Maybe I'll build you a new bed when I come home."

They embrace again. Then she heads off with the horse, he with Innes.

Resolved, Free and Independent States!

The fifth Virginia Convention has been meeting in Williamsburg since May 6, and for most of that time its members have been busy with the court cases of some prominent loyalists, with debating the need to evacuate Norfolk, and, in the absence of royal authority, with other matters of government. Its members are fully aware, however, that they must soon turn to the question of independence. They had been elected that spring amid much discussion of the question. Word has reached Williamsburg of decisions elsewhere: Massachusetts, South Carolina, and Georgia have authorized their delegates in Congress to support measures "for the common good," and it is understood those measures could include independence. North Carolina has been more explicit: its representatives are "to concur with the Delegates of the other Colonies in declaring Independency." America awaits word from Williamsburg.

Finally, on May 13, the Convention begins to debate independence. Some, such as the colony's treasurer, Robert Carter Nicholas, remain worried that the colonies cannot win a war against Britain. Surprisingly, Patrick Henry is also for waiting, at least until the colonies can secure an alliance with France or Spain. Henry is not against independence, but he questions the timing. It falls to Edmund Pendleton, president of the Convention, to reconcile various proposals into a resolution that all, including Nicholas, can support.

The Convention instructs Virginia's delegates in Congress to introduce a motion for independence. Outside the Capitol, Edmund Pendleton, president of the Virginia Convention, reads aloud to the gathered citizens the Preamble and Resolutions of the Virginia Convention, adopted May 15, 1776:

"'Forasmuch as all the endeavours of the United Colonies by the most decent representations and petitions to the king and parliament of Great Britain to restore peace and Security to America under the British government . . . instead of a redress of grievances have produced . . . increased insult oppression and a vigorous attempt to effect our total destruction. By a late act all these colonies are declared to be in rebellion and out of the protection of the British crown our properties subjected to confiscation. . . . Fleets and armies are raised and the aid of foreign troops engaged to assist these destructive purposes: The kings representative in this Colony hath not only withheld all the powers of government from

operating for our safety but . . . is carrying on a piratical and savage war against us tempting our Slaves . . . and training and employing them against their masters. In this state of extreme danger we have no alternative left but an abject submission to the will of those over-bearing tyrants, or a total separation from the crown and government of Great Britain uniting and exerting the strengths of all America for defense and forming alliances with foreign powers for commerce and aid in War: Wherefore appealing to the Searcher of Hearts, . . . and that we are driven . . . by . . . the eternal laws of self-preservation,

"'Resolved, unanimously that the delegates appointed to represent this colony in General Congress be instructed to propose to that respectable body to declare the United Colonies free and independent states absolved from all allegiance to or dependence upon the crown or parliament of Great Britain and that they give the assent of this Colony to such declaration and to whatever measures may be thought proper and necessary by the Congress for forming foreign alliances and a confederation of the colonies . . . : Provided that the power of forming government for and the regulation of the internal concerns of each colony be left to the respective colonial legislatures.

"'Resolved unanimously that a Committee ought to prepare a Declaration of Rights and such a plan of government as will be most likely to maintain peace and order in this colony and secure substantial and equal liberty to the people.'"

Interlude

Following the Virginia Convention's instructions, Richard Henry Lee made the motion for independence in Philadelphia on June 7. About a month later, the Continental Congress adopted the Declaration of Independence.

Back in Williamsburg in the meantime, the work of the Virginia Convention was not done. Having severed Virginia's ties with Great Britain, the Convention appointed a committee to "prepare a Declaration of Rights and such a plan of government as will be most likely to maintain peace and order in this colony and secure substantial and equal liberty to the people." In other words, Virginia had to create a government of its own. And, even before a constitution, the Convention decided, Virginia needed a declaration of rights. Its purpose, Edmund Randolph later explained, was that, "in all the revolutions of time, of human opinion, and of government, a perpetual standard should be erected, around which the people might rally and . . . be forever admonished to be watchful, firm, and virtuous."

Virginia's Declaration of Rights was written largely by George Mason, a delegate from Fairfax County. Among the principles Mason set forth were that all power is derived from the people, that people have the right to a trial by jury, that cruel and unusual punishments ought not to be inflicted, and that there ought to be freedom of the press. The Convention went beyond Mason's call for religious tolerance declaring that all men were entitled to the free exercise of religion.

Virginia's Declaration of Rights, adopted June 12, influenced the marquis de Lafayette in 1789 when he drafted the French Declaration of the Rights of Man and the Citizen and James Madison when, that same year, he drew up the amendments to the Constitution that became America's Bill of Rights. More immediately and most clearly of all, George Mason's Declaration influenced Thomas Jefferson's. Wrote Mason: "All Men are by nature equally free and Independent and have certain inherent Rights . . . namely the enjoyment of Life and liberty . . . and pursuing and obtaining happiness." A month later, Jefferson wrote "that all men are created equal," that they have "certain unalienable Rights, that among these are Life, Liberty and the pursuit of Happiness."

On June 29, the Convention adopted a constitution that established a government for Virginia, one with a governor (whose powers were strictly limited since the colonists recalled all too well Dunmore's abuses and the power of his predecessors), a legislature with two houses, and a court system. The delegates then elected Patrick Henry the first governor of the independent Commonwealth of Virginia. No longer were Virginians subjects of a king; they were now citizens of an independent state. Their rights were not granted by England; these were, as the Declaration of Independence would soon declare, unalienable rights.

FRIDAY, June 14, 1776.

POSTSCRIPT.

No. 72.

IN CONVENTION.

JUNE 12, 1776.

A DECLARATION of RIGHTS made by the representatives of the good people of Virginia, assembled in full and free Convention; which rights do pertain to them, and their posterity, as the basis and foundation of government.

1. THAT all men are by nature equally free and independent, and have certain inherent rights, of which, when they enter into a state of society, they cannot, by any compact, deprive or divest their posterity; namely, the enjoyment of life and liberty, with the means of acquiring and possessing property, and pursuing and obtaining happiness and safety.

2. That all power is vested in, and consequently derived from, the people; that magistrates are their trustees and servants, and at all times amenable to them.

3. That government is, or ought to be, instituted for the common benefit, protection, and security, of the people, nation, or community; of all the various modes and forms of government that is best, which is capable of producing the greatest degree of happiness and safety, and is most effectually secured against the danger of mal-administration; and that whenever any government shall be found inadequate or contrary to these purposes, a majority of the community hath an indubitable, unalienable, and indefeasible right, to reform, alter, or abolish it, in such manner as shall be judged most conducive to the publick weal.

4. That no man, or set of men, are entitled to exclusive or separate emoluments or privileges from the community, but in consideration of publick services; which, not being descendible, neither ought the offices of magistrate, legislator, or judge, to be hereditary.

5. That the legislative and executive powers of the state should be separate and distinct from the judicative; and that the members of the two first may be restrained from oppression, by feeling and participating the burthens of the people, they should, at fixed periods, be reduced to a private station, return into that body from which they were originally taken, and the vacancies be supplied by frequent, certain, and regular elections, in which all, or any part of the former members, to be again eligible, or ineligible, as the laws shall direct.

6. That elections of members to serve as representatives of the people, in assembly, ought to be free; and that all men, having sufficient evidence of permanent common interest with, and attachment to, the community, have the right of suffrage, and cannot be taxed or deprived of their property for publick uses without their own consent, or that of their representatives so elected, nor bound by any law to which they have not, in like manner, assented, for the publick good.

7. That all power of suspending laws, or the execution of laws, by any authority without consent of the representatives of the people, is injurious to their rights, and ought not to be exercised.

8. That in all capital or criminal prosecutions a man hath a right to demand the cause and nature of his accusation, to be

Virginia's Declaration of Rights headlined Alexander Purdie's *Virginia Gazette Postscript* on June 14, 1776. This reproduction was set and printed by Colonial Williamsburg's Printing Office.

VIRGINIA DECLARATION OF RIGHTS

1. THAT all Men are by nature equally free and Independent and have certain inherent Rights of which when they enter into a state of Society they cannot by any compact deprive or divest their Posterity namely the enjoyment of Life and liberty with the means of acquiring and possessing property and pursuing and obtaining happiness and Safety.

2. THAT all power is vested in and consequently derived from the People that Magistrates are their Trustees and Servants and at all times amenable to them.

3. THAT Government is or ought to be instituted for the common benefit protection and Security of the People Nation or Community of all the various Modes and forms of Government that is best which is capable of producing the greatest degree of happiness and Safety and is most effectually secured against the danger of Mal-Administration and that whenever any Government shall be found inadequate or contrary to these purposes a Majority of the Community hath an indubitable unalienable and indefeasible right to reform alter or abolish it in such manner as shall be judged conducive to the publick Weal.

4. THAT no Man or set of Men are intitled to exclusive or separate Emoluments or Privileges from the Community but in consideration of publick Services which not being descendible neither ought the Offices of Magistrate Legislator or Judge to be hereditary.

5. THAT the Legislative and Executive powers of the State should be separate and Distinct from the Judicative and that the Members of the two first may be restrained from oppression by feeling and participating the burthens of the People they should at fixed Periods be reduced to a private station return into the Body from which they were originally taken and the vacancies be supplied by frequent certain and regular Elections in which all or any part of the former Members to be again eligible or ineligible as the laws shall direct.

6. THAT Elections of Members to serve as representatives of the People in Assembly ought to be free and that all Men having sufficient evidence of permanent common Interest with and attachment to the Community have the right of Suffrage and cannot be taxed or deprived of their Property for Publick Uses without their own Consent or that of their Representatives so Elected

nor bound by any Law to which they have not in like manner assented for the public good.

7. THAT all Power of suspending Laws or the execution of Laws by any Authority without consent of the Representatives of the People is injurious to their rights and ought not to be exercised.

8. THAT in all Capital or Criminal Prosecutions a Man hath a right to demand the Cause and Nature of his Accusation to be confronted with the Accusers and Witnesses to call for Evidence in his favour and to a speedy Trial by an impartial Jury of his Vicinage without whose unanimous consent He cannot be found guilty nor can he be compelled to give Evidence against himself that no Man be deprived of his liberty except by the Law of the Land or the Judgment of his Peers.

9. THAT excessive Bail ought not to be required nor excessive Fines imposed nor cruel and unusual Punishments inflicted.

10. THAT General Warrants whereby any Officer or Messenger may be commanded to search suspected places without evidence of a fact committed Or to seize any Person or Persons not named or whose Offence is not particularly described and supported by evidence are grievous and oppressive and ought not to be granted.

11. THAT in Controversies respecting Property and in suits between Man and Man the antient Trial by Jury is preferable to any other and ought to be held sacred.

12. THAT the freedom of the Press is one of the great Bulwarks of liberty and can never be restrained but by despotic Government.

13. THAT a well regulated Militia composed of the Body of the People trained to Arms is the proper natural and safe Defence of a free State that standing Armies in time of peace should be avoided as dangerous to liberty and that in all Cases the Military should be under strict Subordination to and governed by the Civil power.

14. THAT the People have a right to Uniform Government and therefore that no Government separate from or Independent of the Government of Virginia ought to be erected or established within the Limits thereof.

15. THAT no free Government or the Blessing of Liberty can be preserved to any People but by a firm adherence to Justice Moderation Temperance Frugality and Virtue and by frequent recurrence to fundamental Principles.

16. THAT Religion or the Duty which we owe to our Creator and the manner of discharging it can be directed only by reason and Conviction not by force or Violence and therefore all Men are equally intitled to the free exercise of Religion according to the Dictates of Conscience And that it is the mutual Duty of all to practice Christian Forbearance Love and Charity towards each other.

ACT II
Citizens at War
1776~1781

A Declaration of Independence

Richard Henry Lee made the motion on June 7 in Philadelphia "That these United Colonies are, and of right ought to be, free and independent States." The delegates to the Continental Congress, after consulting with their constituents, adopted Lee's resolution. Congress realized a statement was in order to articulate independence for the people of the American colonies and to assert it to Parliament, the king, and the world. To draft such a statement, they appointed a committee that included Thomas Jefferson of Virginia, John Adams of Massachusetts, and Benjamin Franklin of Pennsylvania. It was, of course, Jefferson who wrote the first draft. On July 2, Congress accepted the Declaration of Independence. On July 4, the Declaration of Independence was signed by John Hancock, president of the Congress, and Charles Thomson, its secretary.

Other delegates did not sign until the official, engrossed copy was ready in August, but word of the Declaration spread well before then. On the evening of the fourth, John Dunlap, a Philadelphia printer, began setting type, and the next day copies of his broadside of the Declaration went off by post rider to the assemblies of far-flung states, to their committees of correspondence, and to the commanding officer of the continental troops, George Washington. This was how matters of public importance were made known when news could not travel any faster than a horse could gallop or a ship could sail, when not everyone saw newspapers, and when many who saw them could not read them.

In Philadelphia, the first reading of the printed resolution occurred on July 8, after the Committee of Safety had prepared a suitable celebration. John Nixon, a member of the committee, read it to a throng gathered in the yard of the statehouse, the building that would later be called Independence Hall. The Declaration was read "at the head of each brigade of the continental army posted at and near New York," where it was "every where received with loud huzzas and the utmost demonstrations of joy." That evening in Manhattan's Bowling Green, patriots pulled down the statue of King George, "the just desert [sic] of an ungrateful tyrant," as one newspaper reported. The lead from the statue was melted down to make bullets for the Continental army.

That same day, July 9, Virginians drove Lord Dunmore and the British and their loyalist adherents from their haven on Gwynn's Island. Dunmore's fleet cruised the Potomac River, burning one plantation and terrorizing the area before sailing through the Virginia Capes for New York.

Williamsburg did not receive news of the Declaration for another ten days or so. On July 19, Alexander Purdie reported it in his Virginia Gazette *and printed excerpts of the Declaration. The next day, the rival newspaper published by John Dixon and William Hunter and also called the* Virginia Gazette *carried the full text. On July 22, the Council of State, the only official government body then in session, ordered that the document*

> *be solemnly proclaimed at four oClock in the afternoon on Thursday next at the Capitol in the*
> *City of Williamsburg also at the Court of Hustings, and at the Palace; that the Mayor of the*
> *said City be made acquainted therewith, and requested with the Corporation*
> *to give their attendance.*
>
> *Also that the Commanding Officer of the Continental Forces be informed thereof and desired*
> *to give orders for the Army to parade on that occasion.*

Accordingly, on Thursday, July 25, three weeks after John Hancock signed the Declaration, the words that changed the course of history are read at three locations in Williamsburg. The two Gazettes *report the parading of troops, the booming of cannon, and the firing of muskets throughout the town. The ceremonies and celebrations take place "amidst the acclamations of the people."*

In CONGRESS, July 4, 1776.

The unanimous Declaration of the thirteen united States of America,

When in the Course of human events, it becomes necessary for one people to dissolve the political bands which have connected them with another, and to assume among the powers of the earth, the separate and equal station to which the Laws of Nature and of Nature's God entitle them, a decent respect to the opinions of mankind requires that they should declare the causes which impel them to the separation.

We hold these truths to be self-evident, that all men are created equal, that they are endowed by their Creator with certain unalienable Rights, that among these are Life, Liberty and the pursuit of Happiness.—That to secure these rights, Governments are instituted among Men, deriving their just powers from the consent of the governed, —That whenever any Form of Government becomes destructive of these ends, it is the Right of the People to alter or to abolish it, and to institute new Government, laying its foundation on such principles and organizing its powers in such form, as to them shall seem most likely to effect their Safety and Happiness. Prudence, indeed, will dictate that Governments long established should not be changed for light and transient causes; and accordingly all experience hath shewn, that mankind are more disposed to suffer, while evils are sufferable, than to right themselves by abolishing the forms to which they are accustomed. But when a long train of abuses and usurpations, pursuing invariably

the same Object evinces a design to reduce them under absolute Despotism, it is their right, it is their duty, to throw off such Government, and to provide new Guards for their future security. —Such has been the patient sufferance of these Colonies; and such is now the necessity which constrains them to alter their former Systems of Government. The history of the present King of Great Britain is a history of repeated injuries and usurpations, all having in direct object the establishment of an absolute Tyranny over these States. To prove this, let Facts be submitted to a candid world.

He has refused his Assent to Laws, the most wholesome and necessary for the public good.

He has forbidden his Governors to pass Laws of immediate and pressing importance, unless suspended in their operation till his Assent should be obtained; and when so suspended, he has utterly neglected to attend to them.

He has refused to pass other Laws for the Accommodation of large districts of people, unless those people would relinquish the right of Representation in the Legislature, a right inestimable to them and formidable to tyrants only.

He has called together legislative bodies at places unusual, uncomfortable, and distant from the depository of their public Records, for the sole purpose of fatiguing them into compliance with his measures.

He has dissolved Representative Houses repeatedly, for opposing with manly firmness his invasions on the rights of the people.

He has refused for a long time, after such dissolutions, to cause others to be elected; whereby the Legislative powers, incapable of Annihilation, have returned to the People at large for their exercise; the State remaining in the mean time exposed to all the dangers of invasion from without, and convulsions within.

He has endeavoured to prevent the population of these States; for that purpose obstructing the Laws for Naturalization of Foreigners; refusing to pass others to encourage their migrations hither, and raising the conditions of new Appropriations of Lands.

He has obstructed the Administration of Justice, by refusing his Assent to Laws for establishing Judiciary powers.

He has made Judges dependent on his Will alone, for the tenure of their offices, and the amount and payment of their salaries.

He has erected a multitude of New Offices, and sent hither swarms of Officers to harass our people, and eat out their substance.

He has kept among us, in times of peace, Standing Armies without the Consent of our legislatures.

He has affected to render the Military independent of and superior to the Civil power.

He has combined with others to subject us to a jurisdiction foreign to our constitution, and unacknowledged by our laws; giving his Assent to their Acts of pretended Legislation:

For Quartering large bodies of armed troops among us:

For protecting them, by mock Trial, from punishment for any Murders which they should commit on the Inhabitants of these States:

For cutting off our Trade with all parts of the world:

For imposing Taxes on us without our Consent:

For depriving us in many cases, of the benefits of Trial by Jury:

For transporting us beyond Seas to be tried for pretended Offences:

For abolishing the free System of English Laws in a neighbouring Province, establishing therein an Arbitrary government, and enlarging its Boundaries so as to render it at once an example and fit instrument for introducing the same absolute rule into these Colonies:

For taking away our Charters, abolishing our most valuable Laws, and altering fundamentally the Forms of our Governments:

For suspending our own Legislatures, and declaring themselves invested with power to legislate for us in all cases whatsoever.

He has abdicated Government here, by declaring us out of his Protection and waging War against us.

He has plundered our seas, ravaged our Coasts, burnt our towns, and destroyed the lives of our people.

He is at this time transporting large Armies of foreign Mercenaries to compleat the works of death, desolation and tyranny, already begun with circumstances of Cruelty & perfidy scarcely paralleled in the most barbarous ages, and totally unworthy the Head of a civilized nation.

He has constrained our fellow Citizens taken Captive on the high Seas to bear Arms against their Country, to become the executioners of their friends and Brethren, or to fall themselves by their Hands.

He has excited domestic insurrections amongst us, and has endeavoured to bring on the inhabitants of our frontiers, the merciless Indian Savages, whose known rule of warfare, is an undistinguished destruction of all ages, sexes and conditions.

In every stage of these Oppressions We have Petitioned for Redress in the most humble terms: Our repeated Petitions have been answered only by repeated injury. A Prince whose character is thus marked by every act which may define a Tyrant, is unfit to be the ruler of a free people.

Nor have We been wanting in attentions to our Brittish brethren. We have warned them from time to time of attempts by their legislature to extend an unwarrantable jurisdiction over us. We have reminded them of the circumstances of our emigration and settlement here. We have appealed to their native justice and magnanimity, and we have conjured them by the ties of our common kindred to disavow these usurpations, which, would inevitably interrupt our connections and correspondence. They too have been deaf to the voice of justice and of consanguinity. We must, therefore, acquiesce in the necessity, which denounces our Separation, and hold them, as we hold the rest of mankind, Enemies in War, in Peace Friends.

We, therefore, the Representatives of the united States of America, in General Congress, Assembled, appealing to the Supreme Judge of the world for the rectitude of our intentions, do, in the Name, and by Authority of the good People of these Colonies, solemnly publish and declare, That these United Colonies are, and of Right ought to be Free and Independent States; that they are Absolved from all Allegiance to the British Crown, and that all political connection between them and the State of Great Britain, is and ought to be totally dissolved; and that as Free and Independent States, they have full Power to levy War, conclude Peace, contract Alliances, establish Commerce, and to do all other Acts and Things which Independent States may of right do. And for the support of this Declaration, with a firm reliance on the protection of divine Providence, we mutually pledge to each other our Lives, our Fortunes and our sacred Honor.

IN CONGRESS, JULY 4, 1776.

The unanimous Declaration of the thirteen united States of America.

When in the Course of human events, it becomes necessary for one people to dissolve the political bands which have connected them with another, and to assume among the powers of the earth, the separate and equal station to which the Laws of Nature and of Nature's God entitle them, a decent respect to the opinions of mankind requires that they should declare the causes which impel them to the separation.

We hold these truths to be self-evident, that all men are created equal, that they are endowed by their Creator with certain unalienable Rights, that among these are Life, Liberty and the pursuit of Happiness.—That to secure these rights, Governments are instituted among Men, deriving their just powers from the consent of the governed,—That whenever any Form of Government becomes destructive of these ends, it is the Right of the People to alter or to abolish it, and to institute new Government, laying its foundation on such principles and organizing its powers in such form, as to them shall seem most likely to effect their Safety and Happiness. Prudence, indeed, will dictate that Governments long established should not be changed for light and transient causes; and accordingly all experience hath shewn, that mankind are more disposed to suffer, while evils are sufferable, than to right themselves by abolishing the forms to which they are accustomed. But when a long train of abuses and usurpations, pursuing invariably the same Object evinces a design to reduce them under absolute Despotism, it is their right, it is their duty, to throw off such Government, and to provide new Guards for their future security.—Such has been the patient sufferance of these Colonies; and such is now the necessity which constrains them to alter their former Systems of Government. The history of the present King of Great Britain is a history of repeated injuries and usurpations, all having in direct object the establishment of an absolute Tyranny over these States. To prove this, let Facts be submitted to a candid world.

He has refused his Assent to Laws, the most wholesome and necessary for the public good.

He has forbidden his Governors to pass Laws of immediate and pressing importance, unless suspended in their operation till his Assent should be obtained; and when so suspended, he has utterly neglected to attend to them.

He has refused to pass other Laws for the accommodation of large districts of people, unless those people would relinquish the right of Representation in the Legislature, a right inestimable to them and formidable to tyrants only.

He has called together legislative bodies at places unusual, uncomfortable, and distant from the depository of their public Records, for the sole purpose of fatiguing them into compliance with his measures.

He has dissolved Representative Houses repeatedly, for opposing with manly firmness his invasions on the rights of the people.

He has refused for a long time, after such dissolutions, to cause others to be elected; whereby the Legislative powers, incapable of Annihilation, have returned to the People at large for their exercise; the State remaining in the mean time exposed to all the dangers of invasion from without, and convulsions within.

He has endeavoured to prevent the population of these States; for that purpose obstructing the Laws for Naturalization of Foreigners; refusing to pass others to encourage their migrations hither, and raising the conditions of new Appropriations of Lands.

He has obstructed the Administration of Justice, by refusing his Assent to Laws for establishing Judiciary powers.

He has made Judges dependent on his Will alone, for the tenure of their offices, and the amount and payment of their salaries.

He has erected a multitude of New Offices, and sent hither swarms of Officers to harrass our people, and eat out their substance.

He has kept among us, in times of peace, Standing Armies without the Consent of our legislatures.

He has affected to render the Military independent of and superior to the Civil power.

He has combined with others to subject us to a jurisdiction foreign to our constitution, and unacknowledged by our laws; giving his Assent to their Acts of pretended Legislation:

For quartering large bodies of armed troops among us:

For protecting them, by a mock Trial, from punishment for any Murders which they should commit on the Inhabitants of these States:

For cutting off our Trade with all parts of the world:

For imposing Taxes on us without our Consent:

For depriving us in many cases, of the benefits of Trial by Jury:

For transporting us beyond Seas to be tried for pretended offences:

For abolishing the free System of English Laws in a neighbouring Province, establishing therein an Arbitrary government, and enlarging its Boundaries so as to render it at once an example and fit instrument for introducing the same absolute rule into these Colonies:

For taking away our Charters, abolishing our most valuable Laws, and altering fundamentally the Forms of our Governments:

For suspending our own Legislatures, and declaring themselves invested with power to legislate for us in all cases whatsoever.

He has abdicated Government here, by declaring us out of his Protection and waging War against us.

He has plundered our seas, ravaged our Coasts, burnt our towns, and destroyed the lives of our people.

He is at this time transporting large Armies of foreign Mercenaries to compleat the works of death, desolation and tyranny, already begun with circumstances of Cruelty & perfidy scarcely paralleled in the most barbarous ages, and totally unworthy the Head of a civilized nation.

He has constrained our fellow Citizens taken Captive on the high Seas to bear Arms against their Country, to become the executioners of their friends and Brethren, or to fall themselves by their Hands.

He has excited domestic insurrections amongst us, and has endeavoured to bring on the inhabitants of our frontiers, the merciless Indian Savages, whose known rule of warfare, is an undistinguished destruction of all ages, sexes and conditions.

In every stage of these Oppressions We have Petitioned for Redress in the most humble terms: Our repeated Petitions have been answered only by repeated injury. A Prince, whose character is thus marked by every act which may define a Tyrant, is unfit to be the ruler of a free people.

Nor have We been wanting in attentions to our British brethren. We have warned them from time to time of attempts by their legislature to extend an unwarrantable jurisdiction over us. We have reminded them of the circumstances of our emigration and settlement here. We have appealed to their native justice and magnanimity, and we have conjured them by the ties of our common kindred to disavow these usurpations, which, would inevitably interrupt our connections and correspondence. They too have been deaf to the voice of justice and of consanguinity. We must, therefore, acquiesce in the necessity, which denounces our Separation, and hold them, as we hold the rest of mankind, Enemies in War, in Peace Friends.

We, therefore, the Representatives of the united States of America, in General Congress, Assembled, appealing to the Supreme Judge of the world for the rectitude of our intentions, do, in the Name, and by Authority of the good People of these Colonies, solemnly publish and declare, That these United Colonies are, and of Right ought to be Free and Independent States; that they are Absolved from all Allegiance to the British Crown, and that all political connection between them and the State of Great Britain, is and ought to be totally dissolved; and that as Free and Independent States, they have full Power to levy War, conclude Peace, contract Alliances, establish Commerce, and to do all other Acts and Things which Independent States may of right do.—And for the support of this Declaration, with a firm reliance on the protection of divine Providence, we mutually pledge to each other our Lives, our Fortunes and our sacred Honor.

John Hancock

Button Gwinnett
Lyman Hall
Geo Walton.

Wm Hooper
Joseph Hewes,
John Penn

Edward Rutledge.
Thos Heyward Junr.
Thomas Lynch Junr.
Arthur Middleton

Robt Morris
Benjamin Rush
Benja. Franklin
John Morton
Geo Clymer
Jas Smith.
Geo. Taylor
James Wilson
Geo. Ross
Caesar Rodney
Geo Read
Tho M:Kean

Samuel Chase
Wm Paca
Thos Stone
Charles Carroll of Carrollton

George Wythe
Richard Henry Lee
Th Jefferson
Benja Harrison
Thos Nelson jr.
Francis Lightfoot Lee
Carter Braxton

Wm Floyd
Phil. Livingston
Frans Lewis
Lewis Morris

Richd Stockton
Jno Witherspoon
Fras Hopkinson
John Hart
Abra Clark

Josiah Bartlett
Wm Whipple
Saml Adams
John Adams
Robt Treat Paine
Elbridge Gerry
Step Hopkins
William Ellery
Roger Sherman
Samel Huntington
Wm Williams
Oliver Wolcott
Matthew Thornton

Lady Washington Visits the Capital

George Washington was a famously reluctant leader. He styled himself after Cincinnatus, the Roman hero who saved the Republic but wanted only to return to his farm. He did not want to be king. Nonetheless, Washington was the closest to royalty America had, and so, when the wife of the commander in chief arrived in Williamsburg in August 1777, she received a welcome worthy of a queen.

Martha Dandridge Custis Washington was a formidable figure in her own right. The widow Custis may very well have been the richest woman in Virginia when George Washington courted and married her in 1759. Now she capably manages the plantation at Mount Vernon when her husband is absent, and she is also his frequent companion in camp and sometimes his secretary despite the dangers and discomforts of traveling in the army's train.

As her carriage draws up to the Capitol, she is greeted by a military honor guard and huzzahs from the crowd. After she steps out of the carriage, Mayor Edmund Randolph reads aloud resolutions adopted the previous week by the Williamsburg Common Hall:

"'Resolved unanimously, That the most respectful testimony be presented [Lady Washington] on the occasion, of the high sense this Hall entertains of General Washington's distinguished merit, as the illustrious defender and deliverer of his country.

"'Resolved unanimously, That a golden emblematical medal be prepared, to be presented to the General's lady. . . .

"'Resolved unanimously, That the freedom of this City, be presented to General Washington through his lady: and that the Mayor be desired to wait upon her with the same, and with a copy of these several resolutions.'"

Accepting a medal and certificates from Randolph, Lady Washington addresses the crowd.

"I was blessed to be with the general at the camp at Morristown, in New Jersey, for several weeks earlier this year. You are all acquainted with the difficulties endured by our army through the course of the last year, of the near peril they faced while campaigning in New York. And then, when all appeared to be on the verge of collapse, they accomplished

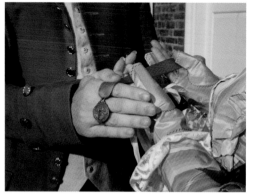

inspired victories at Trenton and at Princeton. I have the pleasure of reporting that through the weeks of late winter and early spring our army has known the chance to heal and repair itself, in preparation of taking up the sword once again to battle the tyrannical intruders that now occupy our countryside. In those weeks at Morristown, enlistments grew at an ever-increasing pace, and of particular gratification is the number of men who decided to remain with the army after their enlistments had ended."

She speaks for her husband: "I know General Washington would expect me to say that any notice that you extend to him he may only accept in recognition that he accomplishes nothing but by the exertions, duty, and sacrifices made by those patriot souls, our men who have committed themselves to take up the sword in defense of our country and the cause of liberty."

Amid cheering, the honor guard fires the cannon. But the realities of the war's miseries cannot be forgotten, and a dirty and grizzled veteran, walking with the aid of a crutch, makes his way through the crowd. He talks of Lady Washington's fine words, calling them a "fitting tribute to a great man, the general," but he cannot conceal his bitterness as he mutters about having nearly died from infection and dysentery and having been promised a pension that he's never received.

"I can tell you that the pension board ain't of the same heart," he cries out. "Don't even seem to want to believe what stares 'em in the face."

He points to his right leg.

"This here, this one will never work again. Happened at Trenton, one of them inspired victories. Be sure, it was a great victory, captured near a thousand Hessians, killed or wounded upwards of a hundred. Wasn't but a handful of us wounded, none killed save the two that froze to death that night in the crossin' of the Delaware. Hades, the battle was a country dance compared to the river crossin'. At least it was until . . . until I took the musket ball in this leg.

"The surgeon done a mighty neat job o' pullin' the ball out clean and sewin' me up," he continues.

"Most times with a wound like this, a man will lose the leg to infection. That surgeon done me right, cleaned it up good, he did. But the leg will never be o' use to me again. I can't work my fields. I can't farm. I can't care for my family."

Lady Washington is paying attention now.

"You are due a pension, good man?" she asks. "Have you applied to the pension board for relief?"

"Aye, ma'am, I have petitioned many times, but I have been refused because I never received any discharge papers."

Randolph explains that there has been great difficulty administering the pensions. Martha Washington looks at the local officials disdainfully and then turns back to the veteran. Answering her questions, he says his name is James Buxton, his regiment was the Fourth Virginia. She has no patience for inefficiency and bureaucracy, and she promises him he will receive his discharge papers. For now, she takes some coins out of her purse and hands them to Buxton. Buxton is reluctant to accept the money.

"I am sorry to have caused . . . ," he begins.

"No," she interrupts. "It is I who am sorry that you have received such ill treatment after giving your country so much."

Near tears, the veteran hobbles off. She watches as he leaves and then turns to the crowd.

"As they sacrifice for us, let us ever determine that we will be committed to their care and well-being on the battlefield. And, for those whose lives are taken in our cause, let us, to our best ability, make certain that their families are protected and preserved. For the men who become wounded, let us be ever vigilant to show them by our continued support the great appreciation that we have for their service and sacrifice."

War in the West

With the end of the French and Indian War in 1763, the British prohibited settlement west of the ridge of the Allegheny Mountains, the so-called Proclamation Line. The hope was to limit conflict with the Indians. In 1774, Lord Dartmouth, the king's secretary of state for the colonies, declared that any attempt to settle these vast regions was "an Act of equal Inhumanity and Injustice to the Indians, that cannot fail to be attended with fatal Consequences." But the promise of that land was too great to resist, and thousands of white settlers made their way into the backcountry.

Among the British who encouraged Indians to harass settlers was Henry Hamilton, the royal lieutenant governor of Detroit in what later became Michigan. Settlers accused him of paying Indians to bring him scalps. His nickname among the settlers, rightly or wrongly, was "the Hair Buyer."

Back in Williamsburg, Governor Patrick Henry and members of the General Assembly sent Lieutenant Colonel George Rogers Clark to defend the West. Clark, too, earned a reputation in some circles as bloodthirsty, or at least a man with a lust for power and fortune. In 1778, Clark's troops seized British outposts at Kaskaskia and Cahokia on the Mississippi River in what is now Illinois. In late February 1779, after marching 180 miles, Clark and his men surprised Hamilton and the British at Vincennes, now in Indiana. Hamilton surrendered. He and his men were marched in irons to Williamsburg where, according to his own account, "a considerable Mob gather'd about us." The governor's council ordered that they be shackled and confined in the jail.

Among those discussing the charges against Hamilton are John Beckley, the clerk of the governor's council, and the distinguished Robert Carter Nicholas, once treasurer of the colony and now a member of the commonwealth's Court of Chancery. Beckley has pointed out the severity of the charges, and Nicholas has noted that there has been no mention of a trial, or even a hearing.

"In truth," Nicholas says, "grave injuries have been committed by both sides. As wise men in every age have observed, in war truth is usually the first victim."

Now the handcuffed Hamilton arrives, accompanied by his military guard and assorted locals who are harassing and taunting him. Seeing Nicholas, they fall silent. Hamilton, looking tired but dignified, addresses the clerk to protest how he is being treated. He has signed Clark's articles of capitulation, and the actions of his captors are, he feels, "a reproach to all accepted sanctions for prisoners of war." He has been given no chance to confront his accusers, he has been transported to Williamsburg in irons, he has been relieved of documents and papers that he believes will exonerate him, and he understands that he is not only to be confined but also shackled.

"I am sure," responds Beckley, an ardent patriot, "that a day of reckoning is soon at hand."

The townspeople cheer and jeer.

Nicholas cautions the younger man: "Mr. Beckley, I advise that you not exceed yourself, sir."

Beckley nonetheless proceeds to remind Hamilton that he held a council of war with the chiefs of the Shawnee, the Delaware, the Huron, the Ottawa, and others. Hamilton retorts that Virginians have negotiated with the Cherokee and Catawba.

"Well, now, do I understand that our crime is friendship and alliance with the Indian nations of the Ohio and Illinois? If that be the case, how different is it from those that Virginia has made with the Cherokee and Catawba? Your own Governor Henry treated with the Cherokee here in Williamsburg near about the same time, did he not?"

But, Beckley argues, Hamilton not only supplied the Indians with a feast but with guns, ammunition, and other weapons. Hamilton answers that he is a British official charged to do all in his power to end an insurrection. He has followed the accepted features of warfare.

"The incitement of allies to murder, to butchery, is not an accepted feature of warfare, sir," says Beckley. "The paying of bounties for scalps is not recognized, sir."

Measured but vehement, Hamilton denies the charges: "Murder, pillage, and scalp taking have never been done upon my order or with any prior knowledge on my part or, so far as I am aware, with any knowledge on the part of my officers."

Hamilton now relates what occurred during the American siege of Fort Sackville at Vincennes on the day before his surrender.

"About two o'clock in the afternoon, an Indian party of some sixteen men had returned to town from scouting. Seeing the English flag over the fort, and not being aware of the rebel force, they discharged their firelocks, their custom for saluting us and announcing their presence. Clark instantly sent seventy of his men against them. Two were killed on the spot; another escaped wounded. The rest were bound and brought to the fort where they were set in a circle before the gate. All of this, you understand, occurred under a flag of truce. Clark then gave the order, and each Indian, as he sat there upon the ground with his hands bound, was in turn tomahawked in the head. Once we were taken prisoners, Clark ordered the scalps of the slaughtered Indians to be hung up by our tents.

"In the evening," Hamilton continues, "Colonel Clark ordered neck irons, fetters, and handcuffs to be made for those officers who had been employed as partisans with the Indians. He said he had made a vow never to spare woman or child of the Indians or those who were employed with them.

"Do not speak to me of atrocities, young man," concludes Hamilton.

Amid embarrassed silence, Hamilton is taken back to the jail.

In Desperate Circumstance

Jane Vobe, mistress of the King's Arms Tavern, knows well about the war at home: provisions are hard to come by, but so are guests. There are few travelers now to seek lodging. Gone are the debaters and revelers who once filled Williamsburg's taverns. Only one sort of person seems on the increase: beggars. One approaches Mrs. Vobe now, her filthy dress in tatters, her face smudged with soot and dirt.

"Mrs. Vobe? Mistress? Please. Might I speak with you?"

"I cannot spare anything," answers Mrs. Vobe. "Times is hard everywhere, and here's no different. I have no food to give you or those like you. I need what little I have for my patrons and my household. I've nothin' to spare."

"Mrs. Vobe! I do not come to you for your pity. I come to you as a familiar face, hoping that your Christian nature will allow you to provide work for me so I may feed and care for myself. Do you not recognize me?"

"I do not. And it would not make a difference if I did," says the tavern keeper, turning on her heel.

"I am Barbry Hoy, wife of Alexander Hoy, the carpenter."

The words freeze Mrs. Vobe. She turns back.

"Mrs. Hoy? Alexander's wife? My God, where have you been?"

Barbry Hoy tells her of her trials and odyssey these last four years. Alexander Hoy enlisted in the army so that he could feed his family with the bonus offered recruits and in hopes of a bounty in western land whenever the war should end. In the spring of 1780, he was at Charleston, South Carolina, when the British besieged the city. Word has already reached Williamsburg of the disaster that befell the Continental army there, and in particular the Virginians.

General William Woodford had marched south from New Jersey in answer to true reports that the British would invade the southern colonies. Along the way he had been joined by detachments of Virginia volunteers. Woodford's army reinforced the garrison at Charleston. But the British had massed ten thousand troops around the city and sealed off all access save for the road by which the patriots arrived. Trapped and bombarded, the patriots asked to negotiate, but the British refused. On

May 12, the patriots surrendered. The prisoners were kept aboard ships far worse than any jail on land. Each day, more bodies were tossed into the water.

As for Barbry Hoy, she had stayed behind in Williamsburg, working the small farm with her daughters and one aged slave. But the crops were poor, and there was hardly a market or way to reach it safely. When pensions for servicemen's families ran out in 1779, she sold old Henry, and, when that pittance was gone, she sent her daughters into domestic service, first Mary, then Lizzie. Better that than have them join her in following the army.

"I thank God I did not take the girls to be camp followers," she tells Mrs. Vobe. "No one cares a whit about camp followers, mistress. We lived very poor. We scrounged for food. We had little protection from the weather. We earned rations and a little coin doing laundry, sometimes cooking for the officers, nursing the injured, and so many sick . . . so many fall sick. I had to watch so many men die from wounds of battle, but so many more were killed by the dysentery and camp fevers—and not just the men. Them dangers we all shared, man, woman, and child."

When Charleston fell, Mrs. Hoy joined three other wives and headed back toward Virginia. Two were murdered by deserters; one wandered away. Mrs. Hoy continued on, hoping for word of her husband, praying for news.

"He is a prisoner, maybe, on one of those horrid prison ships in the Charleston harbor," she tells Mrs. Vobe. "I do not know. I only have this."

She shows Mrs. Vobe a scrap of dirty paper to which she has been clinging. Unable to read it, she asks Mrs. Vobe to do so.

"Mrs. Vobe, you may find his name quick," she pleads. "Read the lists. Find my Alexander."

Mrs. Vobe reads:

"We have the honor of enclosing you a copy of a letter . . . which was handed [to] us immediately on our being put on board this ship. . . . We . . . beg leave to observe, that should it fall to the lot of all, or any of us, to be made victims, . . . we have only to regret that our blood cannot be disposed of more to the advancement of the glorious cause to which we have adhered. A separate roll of our names attend this letter.

With the greatest respect, we are, sir,

Your most obedient and humble servants,

STEPHEN MOORE, Lieut. Col. N[orth] Carolina Militia.

JOHN BARNWELL, Major So[uth] Carolina Militia,

for ourselves and 130 prisoners."

Mrs. Vobe studies the list.

"Forgive me, Mrs. Hoy, but your husband's name is not on this roll."

"But it could be," Barbry Hoy interjects with surprising energy. "His name could be on the list, on another list. He could be a prisoner on one of those ships."

Gently, Mrs. Vobe suggests, "It might be better if he were not."

"I know that."

Mrs. Vobe now tells Mrs. Hoy that the scullery needs attending and that in return she can have a place to rest for the night.

"Just for tonight, you understand. Go round back and wait for me. I wish I could do more."

The Town Is Taken

Fearing Williamsburg was not safe from the British, in April 1780 the government moved upriver to Richmond. It turned out that neither place was safe. The British invaded the new capital first, inflicting heavy damage on Richmond in January 1781. In April, British forces attacked the American position on the James River, east of Williamsburg. The Americans under Colonel James Innes retreated through Williamsburg, taking with them the wounded and supplies. On April 20, the British entered the city. When the victors paraded down Duke of Gloucester Street, at their head rode Major General William Phillips and Brigadier General Benedict Arnold, once a famous patriot and now an infamous traitor to the American cause.

Arnold first made a name for himself early in the war with key roles in pivotal victories against the British at Fort Ticonderoga and Saratoga. Twice wounded, Arnold was admired and trusted for his brave service. Promoted to brigadier general, he was accused of mishandling funds and passed over for key assignments. Arnold grew bitter. He complained to Washington about the "ungrateful returns I have received from my countrymen." He lobbied for and won command of the fort at West Point, the bastion overlooking the Hudson River. For several months in late 1780, Arnold engaged in secret negotiations with Major John Andre, adjutant general of the main British army in New York and a friend of Arnold's wife Peggy. Andre offered Arnold twenty thousand pounds and a commission if he would surrender the fort. Arnold agreed, but American pickets captured Andre and found papers hidden in his boot that revealed the plot. Andre was hanged as a spy, and Arnold fled to a British warship.

With the British approaching, people are running from person to person, store to store. Hopes and fears and rumors spread quickly: "The war is almost over!" "General Arnold is marching on Williamsburg." "Where is General Washington?" "Has he surrendered?" "Where is Governor Jefferson?" "Where is General Lafayette?" "Please let this war be over!"

One thing is certain: the invading army would have looked resplendent to the citizens of Williamsburg. General Arnold himself arrives at the Capitol. He reins in his mount and addresses the crowd.

"Countrymen of British Virginia, hear our news. We come in peace to bring you peace. The rebel insurrection is all but ended. The royal dominion of Virginia is secure."

A townsperson asks Arnold whether, as they have heard, he has burned Richmond.

"During our campaign we did liberate Richmond," Arnold answers. "There was no resistance by Continental forces or militia."

Arnold adds that Thomas Jefferson, who he sneeringly refers to as "your governor," fled across the James River without even a call to arms and that the British burned only warehouses that held rebel munitions or goods.

"Arnold, you're a traitor!" comes a shout from the crowd.

Soldiers try to locate the voice.

Arnold continues, "People of Williamsburg, loyal subjects, you have been misled, just as I was." The Continental army, he tells them, is a shambles and on the edge of mutiny.

"Do not dare dishonor our husbands and sons who serve, sir!" This from a woman wearing a cockaded bonnet and a threadbare gown.

Arnold's tone is firm but understanding: "Madam, I am one who honors the American soldier most. But the rebel army is in such a degraded state that it can hardly keep to the field. Some men are as old as sixty, some young as fourteen. Your own General Anthony Wayne has called these men 'food for worms.'"

A townsman shouts, "You desire our trust, sir, but you insult us!"

Arnold now tells of the British victory last May at Charleston where Americans were besieged by a force twice their size and the Continental Congress attempted no support or reinforcements.

"How could this have happened?" asks Arnold. His answer: "General Lincoln was betrayed by the rebel government."

From the crowd comes another cry of traitor, but it does not faze Arnold for long.

"You own *me* to be a traitor? You, and I, were persuaded to rebel because of the supposed injustice delivered to us by faraway lords, yet nearer lords deliver worse injustice! The economy is ruined. We have no imports or exports. Our money is worthless. Our larders are empty. We have been misled."

Again, there is a call of traitor. This time soldiers level their muskets. But Arnold continues and the moment passes.

"I love my country as do you, sir. I served her supposed 'independence' for five years. I was shot twice. I have suffered wounds, deprivation, and hardship for my country—this country. Yet I have the courage to recognize betrayal."

Arnold's aide now informs the public that Lord North and Parliament, upon instructions from His Majesty the King, have assured that all demands made by the first Congress of his colonies in North America will be met and honored and that there will be no legislation or taxation upon these colonies from Parliament.

"Our liberty is assured, my countrymen! The war is ending!" Arnold declares. He hands a British flag to a soldier and orders him to see it is immediately raised.

Running to Freedom

The British have occupied Williamsburg since June. Now, with Cornwallis preparing to leave for Yorktown, the enslaved people of Williamsburg must decide whether they should leave with them. As British troops headed from the Carolinas into Virginia, more than six hundred former slaves left their rebel masters and followed the troops. The enslaved people of Williamsburg recognize that this may be the best chance for freedom they will ever have.

Should they trust the promises of Cornwallis? A woman and man, Eve from the Randolph household and Juba from the Raleigh Tavern, discuss their options.

"All I'm saying," says Eve, "is that this is our way to freedom. This is what we been waiting for."

"I don't know for sure," answers Juba, "but this don't look like nothing but another way to use the Negroes to stir up some foolishness. I don't like it one bit."

"What of freedom? You don't like that neither?"

"Free to follow the army. Free to hope they don't cast you off to the side when they finished with you. At least here I know I have food to eat. I have clothes to put on."

"That food, it ain't yours. Them clothes, them ain't yours neither. Juba, if I didn't know better, I'd think you was pleased to be a slave."

Kate, a tavern worker like Juba, arrives and passes on the latest reports: one woman has decided to stay and asks that they pray for her; one man has gone with his master to join Washington's army.

None of this sways Eve, who plans to leave with her son George. Kate asks whether she really thinks the British will give her freedom.

"All I know is that freedom won't come to those who wait on it," Eve answers. "I been waiting. I just want to raise my boy, see him grow to be a man, and not worry 'bout no man taking him from me."

"Except the British," interjects Juba. "I never thought that you would be foolish enough to fall prey to the foolish notion of the British freeing Negroes. Hell, they was the ones who brought Negroes here to be slaves! Now they free us? Kate, c'mon, let's go back to the tavern before they start looking for us and thinking we ran off."

Seeing she can't sway Juba, Eve turns to Kate. She reminds her of the times they have spent together, and she talks about how glorious freedom will be. But Kate says she has other things to think about.

"What could possibly sway you from wanting your freedom?" asks Eve.

Nervously, Kate tells her she hasn't been feeling well lately and that she is pregnant. "I'm just so scared."

"If you stay here," Eve warns Kate, "that child will grow up to scrub floors and empty pots of some master or other."

Now Eve realizes Kate won't come.

"I can only hope that God would open the eyes of the white gentlemen, when they are so much engaged for liberty, to think of the state of Negroes," she says. "I'll pray for you—and for that child of yours."

With that, Eve rushes off.

The Promised Land

Gowan Pamphlet was an African-American Baptist preacher and a slave of tavern keeper Jane Vobe. Pamphlet's ministry at first took place largely in secret since laws prohibited large gatherings of blacks. He would often preach in wooded areas, sometimes hidden in arbors made of saplings and underbrush. At some point during or after the Revolution, he began preaching more openly.

Today, taking his text from Deuteronomy, he describes how Moses led his people through the wilderness to the Jordan River but foretells that he will not cross over with them and that Joshua will lead them to the Promised Land.

"'And Moses went and spake these words unto all Israel,'" he reads from his Bible.

"'The Lord thy God, he will go over before thee, and he will destroy these nations from before thee, and thou shalt possess them. . . .

"'And the Lord shall give them up before your face, that ye may do unto them according unto all the commandments which I have commanded you.

"'Be strong and of a good courage, fear not, nor be afraid of them: for the Lord thy God, he it is that doth go with thee; he will not fail thee, nor forsake thee.'

"Brothers and sisters, I don't know," intones the preacher. "Could we be movin' closer to that Promised Land, or at least to the end of the war? God only knows, and he will reveal it by and by. We're all mighty tired of this war, ready to be rid of it. And, if this be the end, do we now stand on Jordan's bank? Can we see that Promised Land just on the other side?"

For years, Pamphlet and his congregation have met in secret. With America's Revolution, he is hopeful that those days are coming to an end. Under British rule, the Church of England was the established church of the colonies, and the only official place to worship in Williamsburg was in Bruton Parish Church. And, says Pamphlet, "There be no speakin' to the Spirit" at Bruton Parish Church.

There are cries of "Amen!" and Pamphlet continues.

"The priest be the only one talkin', and then mostly with his nose down on a paper, readin' some sermon he copied from a book. The only noise the congregation makes is when they recite some tired prayer or sing a sleepy psalm. And you sure wouldn't be listenin' to no black Baptist preacher proclaiming the word!"

But Pamphlet wonders what will happen if the Americans win the

73

war? He has heard that some, like Governor Thomas Jefferson, want people to follow God the way their hearts tell them.

A Baptist preacher and army chaplain, James Ireland, works his way through the crowd. He seconds Pamphlet's thoughts.

"That's right, Preacher Gowan," shouts Ireland. "When Virginia declared independence and made her new government, she wrote a declaration of rights, and one of those rights they declared was that all men are entitled to the free exercise of religion, according to the dictates of conscience. And that it is the mutual duty of all to practice Christian forbearance, love, and charity toward each other."

Pamphlet agrees: "In the Promised Land, we do right because it's right to do, because we

understand and cherish God's law, not because the laws o' men tell us it's right."

A young white militiaman, Gabriel Maupin, has been trying to sort out the messages from Pamphlet and Ireland. Although there are no white members in Gowan Pamphlet's congregation, some Baptist churches serve mixed races, and whites listen in to Pamphlet's sermons occasionally.

"The government has always told us what to do," Maupin says. "Don't we need its guidance?"

"We've now adopted a republican form of government," answers Ireland, "meaning that the people are sovereign, that we govern ourselves, which means we must be wise and act wise if we are to stay free."

"Young sir, you listen to me," says Pamphlet. "It might seem a mess, but that is divine providence. He gave you a will to learn and decide. Now, you been coming round to hear me preach since you was a tadpole. For the last six years, since the war started, you ain't had to sneak to it."

He looks into Maupin's face.

"What if it was to go back like it was: for a man to preach, he had to have a license, he had to be studied, he had to be white. What if they was to say that Gowan couldn't preach no more?"

While Maupin ponders that, Ireland solemnly informs the company that General Washington, whose men have now replaced Cornwallis's in Williamsburg will soon address the troops.

Maupin gathers his kit and heads off to join his unit. Then he turns back and addresses Pamphlet.

"'Be strong and of a good courage, fear not, nor be afraid of them . . .'"

"'. . . for the Lord thy God, he it is that doth go with thee,'" answers the preacher.

"I'll see you in the Promised Land," says Maupin, who then rushes off.

Pamphlet asks Ireland, "When we gets to this Promised Land, how long do you think it'll be to see the end of slavery?"

"In God's time," answers Ireland, "it will be accomplished."

On to Yorktown

*A*mong those Washington trusted most was the marquis de Lafayette, who was just nineteen years old when he volunteered to fight for American liberte! *(This was a cause he would later champion in his own country during the French Revolution.) Early in 1781, in a move to counter the British moves in the South, Washington had ordered Lafayette, now a major general, to march from New York to defend Virginia. There, Lafayette played cat and mouse with Cornwallis, baiting him but not engaging forces that greatly outnumbered his. (Lafayette had about seven thousand men to Cornwallis's twelve thousand.) Cornwallis, energized by victories in Carolina and taunted by the upstart Frenchman, purportedly wrote, "The boy cannot escape me."*

In reality, it would be Cornwallis who could not escape. In early August, looking for a defensible position near the Chesapeake Bay, Cornwallis moved his troops from Williamsburg to Yorktown. There he awaited the reinforcements that he expected to reach him by sea. Meanwhile, Washington himself was en route from New Jersey and bent on uniting all his forces to meet Cornwallis. He sent frequent dispatches to his commanders, urging them to converge on the Tidewater region of Virginia. To his second-in-command, General Benjamin Lincoln, Washington wrote: "Every day we loose [sic] now, is comparatively an age. . . . Hurry on then . . . with your Troops upon the wing of Speed." And to Lafayette: "I hope you will keep Lord Cornwallis safe, without Provisions or Forage untill we arrive."

Washington arrived in Williamsburg on September 14. Lafayette rode up and embraced the commander in chief "with an ardor not easily described," Williamsburg's St. George Tucker wrote to his wife. A few days later, Washington met with the French Admiral de Grasse aboard his flagship Ville de Paris. *De Grasse's fleet had chased the British fleet from the Chesapeake Bay. Washington saw that, if the British could not reinforce Cornwallis by sea, the British would be trapped in Yorktown.*

Seven years earlier Virginia had been the keystone in the debate over declaring independence. The movement could not have proceeded without her peerless talents: Henry the firebrand, Mason the constitutionalist, Randolph the presider, Jefferson the writer, Washington the soldier. Now Virginia has again become the central battleground. Washington knows that, and Cornwallis knows it. Benedict Arnold knows it, but, to his chagrin, he has been ordered north. All the patriots know it, too.

It is the day to march to Yorktown. A crowd has gathered near the courthouse. Hope is on every face, and worry. Washington and Lafayette arrive on horseback. They dismount at the courthouse and make their way up the steps amid huzzahs from the crowd.

Washington addresses the crowd. He recalls the long and bloody six years that have brought his armies to this point, and he credits not himself but the gracious interposition of an overruling Providence. He calls the perseverance of the United States armies through every possible suffering and discouragement little short of a miracle. The veterans have endured hunger, nakedness, and cold and have suffered and bled.

"The value of our liberty will thus be enhanced in our estimation by the difficulty of its attainment," he says and then reminds the crowd that "liberty is not yet secure for our posterity."

"The hour is upon us in which the honor and success of this army as well as the safety of our poor bleeding nation may well depend," the general proclaims. "Lord Cornwallis and his command are trapped at Yorktown with no means of escape or resupply."

Washington continues, "We will march on Yorktown, where I have no doubt but by the blessings of heaven that we shall repel our cruel invaders and see peace and liberty once more returned to these shores, on a more permanent foundation. The game is yet in our own hands; to play it well is all we have to do. I trust that the goodness of the cause and the exertions of the people under divine protection will give us that honorable peace for which we are contending and that soon we shall be enabled to return to our private stations in the bosom of a free, peaceful, and happy country."

Amid huzzahs Washington rides off toward Yorktown.

Epilogue

BENEDICT ARNOLD (1741–1801), whose strategic acumen was responsible for both American and British victories, sailed for London in December 1781. There he met with British officials, including King George III, and tried to convince them not to give up, despite the defeat at Yorktown. He returned to North America to pursue various ventures in New Brunswick, but ultimately he and his wife, Peggy, settled in London.

JOHN BECKLEY (1757–1807) continued to be a key supporter of Jefferson, just as he was during the imprisonment of Henry Hamilton. During Jefferson's presidential campaigns, Beckley served as his campaign manager (though the term didn't exist in the early days of party politics) and wrote a pamphlet, *Address to the People of the United States: with an Epitome and Vindication of the Public Life and Character of Thomas Jefferson*, that was in a sense the first campaign biography. Jefferson rewarded him by appointing him the first librarian of Congress.

JACK BURGESS (dates unknown) worked for James Southall, owner of the Raleigh Tavern, according to Southall's account books, between 1772 and 1775. Those are the last mentions of him in local records.

JAMES BUXTON (dates unknown), who was wounded at Trenton in December 1776 while serving in the Fourth Virginia Regiment, began receiving a pension—thirty-four years later—of $48 a year.

GEORGE ROGERS CLARK (1752–1818), partly because Virginia failed to pay him fully for his years of service, fell deeply into debt, drank heavily, and became involved, despite the opposition of President Washington, in schemes aimed at seizing Spanish land west of the Mississippi River. Clark is still remembered for his daring exploits in the Northwest, though not as widely as his brother William, who along with Meriwether Lewis led America's most famous westward expedition.

CHARLES CORNWALLIS (1738–1805), despite his defeat at Yorktown, continued to be highly regarded by the British government as a soldier and an administrator. As governor-general of India between 1786 and 1793, he secured for England much new territory, and in 1798 he suppressed a French-inspired rebellion in Ireland. He also helped negotiate peace in Europe during the Napoleonic Wars.

EDITH CUMBO (dates unknown), a free black woman who worked at the Raleigh Tavern, appears in a 1778 court record indicating that she was the plaintiff in a trespass, assault, and battery case. In the first census of the United Stated (taken in the year 1790), she is listed among the heads of families for the City of Williamsburg with a household that consisted of two black persons, herself and one other not named. The word "free" is written by her name.

LORD DUNMORE, JOHN MURRAY (1730–1809), after issuing his emancipation proclamation in 1775, setting fire to Norfolk, and pillaging along the Potomac River, sailed through the Virginia Capes and returned to England in 1776. He was reelected to the House of Lords and in 1781 sailed for Virginia in command of a naval expedition whose mission was to recapture Virginia. At sea, he learned of Cornwallis's surrender so went instead to New York, where he called for raising an army of blacks and loyalists. Later he was royal governor of the Bahamas, where he appointed loyalists to government positions and granted tracts of lands to many others. Fifty years after her birth in Williamsburg, Dunmore's daughter Lady Virginia Murray filed a claim against Virginia based on her assertion that the General Assembly sitting at the time of her birth and christening had requested that she be their goddaughter and proposed providing for her in a manner suitable to such an honor. The Commonwealth denied her claim.

EVE (dates unknown) ran away with her son George, most probably when the British occupied Williamsburg in 1781. In an inventory of Peyton Randolph's property, Betty Randolph wrote "gone to the enemy" above the names of thirteen slaves including Eve and George. Eve must have later been recaptured since Betty Randolph's will includes the line that "Eve's bad behaviour laid me under the necessity of selling her." Betty Randolph probably sold Eve to her nephew Harrison Randolph, and Eve again ran away, judging from a 1782 advertisement in which Harrison Randolph offered to pay twenty dollars to anyone apprehending her.

HENRY HAMILTON (ca. 1734–1796) was held without trial in Williamsburg and then Chesterfield for eighteen months. In 1780, he was freed as part of a prisoner exchange. He later became lieutenant governor of Quebec and governor of Bermuda (the capital of which was named for him).

JOSHUA HARDCASTLE (dates unknown) had his "promise that he never would be guilty of a like offence" published in the *Virginia Gazette*s of September 7 and September 9, 1775, along with an account of trial, "as a warning to those who may hereafter sport with the great and glorious cause of America." On November 1, 1776, the *Gazette* reported that Hardcastle expected "to leave this Continent within ten Days." Apparently, he delayed, since a May 9, 1777, *Gazette* reported he intended "to leave the Country immediately."

PATRICK HENRY (1736–1799), famed for oratory such as "If this be treason, make the most of it" and "Give me liberty, or give me death," became the first governor of the Commonwealth of Virginia in July 1776. He was elected to three consecutive one-year terms and then served again from 1784 to 1786. He was later at odds with many of his fellow Revolutionaries, partly because Henry believed the Constitution gave the federal government too much power and did not explicitly protect individual rights. (Several states' delegates delayed voting for ratification until they were assured that a bill of rights would be enacted as soon as the new Congress met.) Still, even a political friend-turned-foe like Edmund Randolph said of Henry that, "for grand impressions in the defense of liberty, the Western world has not yet been able to exhibit a rival."

ALEXANDER HOY (unknown–ca. 1782) returned to Williamsburg sometime after the American defeat at Charleston, South Carolina, and was reunited with his wife, Barbry, and his daughters, Mary and Elizabeth. Although listed as the head of a household composed of six persons in 1782, Alexander died about that time, possibly because of an injury or disease suffered during his military service. Alexander's regiment had probably first gone north to reinforce

General Washington, turning south in 1779 to join the siege at Charleston in 1780. Hoy's daughters, Mary and Elizabeth, lived to adulthood and may have claimed the land bounty due to Alexander for his service to the Continental army.

BARBRY HOY (dates unknown) was forced to turn to the government for assistance. A local court stepped in, recording that "Barbara the wife of Alexander Hoy a poor Soldier in the Service of the Commonwealth is allowed twelve pounds towards the support of herself and Children she being unable to provide for them." Again, in 1779, she received forty pounds as the "wife of a Soldier in the service of the Continent." After the death of her husband, she continued to live in the area for several years. Account books and personal property tax lists show that, as a widow, Hoy was the head of a household that grew to include three persons in addition to herself and her daughters. She paid personal property tax on one free worker in 1783, possibly a kinsman, named William Hoy. In 1785, she borrowed money from her landlord, this time to pay what she still owed for Alexander's burial.

JAMES INNES (1754–1798) rose to the rank of major and fought in numerous battles. He rallied American troops during their 1777 attack on the British at Germantown, Pennsylvania, and he led militia forces after the British invaded Virginia in 1781. After the Revolution, he continued to live in Williamsburg, though his house had been damaged by the war. As Virginia's attorney general, Innes supported the adoption of the federal Constitution. Patrick Henry (who opposed the Constitution) described Innes's oratory as "splendid, magnificent and sufficient to shake the human mind": high praise from the man who was himself known as the "trumpet of the Revolution."

JAMES IRELAND (1748–1806), though persecuted—and jailed—for preaching as a Baptist, a dissenter from the state church in Virginia, before the Revolution, continued to preach, including to troops during the Revolution. He founded churches in various Virginia counties, including Shenandoah, where he died.

THOMAS JEFFERSON (1743–1826) succeeded Patrick Henry as the second governor of an independent Virginia and John Adams as the third president of the United States. As governor, Jefferson was caught off guard by the 1780 British invasion of Virginia, and many, in Virginia and in Congress, criticized him for letting Benedict Arnold's forces take Richmond without a fight. Near his death, in 1826, he asked that he be remembered on his tombstone for three achievements: founding the University of Virginia and authoring the Declaration of Independence and the Virginia Statute for Religious Freedom. Jefferson and John Adams died within hours of one another on July 4.

JUBA (dates unknown) was an enslaved man owned by James Southall, owner of the Raleigh Tavern. Like many other enslaved people, the historical record tells us little of his life.

KATE (dates unknown), like Juba, was an enslaved tavern worker whose fate we do not know. She appears on James Southall's personal property lists of 1783, 1784, and 1786.

MARQUIS DE LAFAYETTE (1757–1834), who was just nineteen years old when he joined the American Revolution, helped win French support for the cause and played a crucial role trapping the British at the Battle of Yorktown. Back in France after the American Revolution, he drafted a Declaration of the Rights of Man and the Citizen, which was in many ways to the French Revolution what Jefferson's Declaration of Independence was to the American. He eventually fell out of favor with more radical revolutionaries and fled to Austria, but he was captured by the

Austrian army and imprisoned for more than five years. When Napoleon came to power, Lafayette returned to France. In 1824, at the invitation of Congress, Lafayette returned to America where he was celebrated as one of the last of the Founding Fathers. In Williamsburg, he stayed at what had been Peyton Randolph's home and attended a banquet and ball held in his honor.

RICHARD HENRY LEE (1732–1794) was a signer of the Declaration of Independence, a document that resulted from his motion for independence. Lee opposed ratification of the federal Constitution, but he served as senator from Virginia in the first Congress under it.

GEORGE MASON (1725–1792) was a leading opponent of the federal Constitution, partly because it allowed the continuation of the slave trade and partly because it did not include a bill of rights guaranteeing the freedoms in the Virginia Declaration of Rights. After Mason's death, Jefferson called him "a man of the first order of wisdom among those who acted on the theatre of the revolution, of expansive mind, profound judgment, cogent in argument, learned in the lore of our former constitution, and earnest for the republican change on democratic principles."

GABRIEL MAUPIN (1737–1800) worked as a saddler and harnessmaker, a tavern keeper, and keeper of the magazine during and probably after the Revolution.

ROBERT CARTER NICHOLAS (1728–1780) worked to prevent violence and never advocated independence, but his legal skill and unquestioned integrity made him a respected leader in Virginia before and during the Revolution. His son-in-law Edmund Randolph described him as "benevolent and liberal" but conceded he appeared "haughty and austere." Nicholas was elected president of the Virginia Convention in 1775, and he was appointed treasurer in 1776 and to the Court of Chancery in 1778. During the war, Nicholas moved his family to the safety of his plantation in Hanover County, where he died. His widow, Anne Nicholas, returned to Williamsburg and died in 1786.

MANN PAGE (1749–1803), after serving one term in the Continental Congress, returned to his plantation near Fredericksburg.

GOWAN PAMPHLET (by 1748–ca. 1807) continued to preach to blacks, mostly enslaved, despite the risk to both the preacher and his congregants. He probably moved with Jane Vobe in 1786 when she relocated her tavern from Williamsburg to Manchester, across the James River from Richmond. He was back in Williamsburg in 1791 with his new owner, David Miller, an employee of Vobe's who bought or inherited him from her estate. During the summer of 1793, Pamphlet was accused of being a messenger in a network of armed slaves. The rumors died down, and in September Miller drew up a deed to set him free. That same year, Pamphlet's church, now numbering about five hundred, became a member of the white-run Dover Baptist Association, a regional organization. Late in Pamphlet's ministry, his services were held in a wooden carriage house in Williamsburg. He died a free man and owner of part of a lot in Williamsburg and fourteen acres about two miles from downtown Williamsburg in James City County.

EDMUND PENDLETON (1721–1803), despite often criticizing Patrick Henry as too radical, drafted the instructions to Virginia's representatives in Congress "to declare the United Colonies free and independent states." After Virginia became independent, Pendleton served as the first Speaker of its House of Delegates and as president of Virginia's Supreme Court of Appeals. He later was president of Virginia's ratifying convention, in which capacity he strongly supported the federal Constitution. He turned down several federal government positions offered by George Washington.

ARIANA RANDOLPH (1730–1801) left for England with her husband, John, in 1775. She never returned to America, even though her husband's body was brought back to Virginia for burial. Ariana Randolph died in London.

EDMUND RANDOLPH (1753–1813) joined the Continental army without his father's knowledge and served as aide-de-camp to George Washington. His loyalist father, John, reacted by writing: "For Gods Sake return to your Family & indeed to yourself." Edmund married Elizabeth Nicholas, daughter of Robert Carter Nicholas, despite political and religious differences between their families that, according to Randolph, led to "increasing rancour" and made the marriage seem "an impossibility." Randolph served as delegate to the fifth Virginia Convention (representing Williamsburg), mayor of Williamsburg, attorney general of Virginia, governor of Virginia, delegate to the Continental Congress and to the Constitutional Convention, attorney general of the United States, and secretary of state of the United States. Randolph's government service came to an end in 1795 when the British intercepted a letter from a French minister. The letter seemed to show that Randolph had asked for a bribe. He was almost certainly innocent of that charge. Even Randolph's own efforts to vindicate himself, however, demonstrated that he had made improper and embarrassing comments to the French minister about those in Washington's administration who were more supportive of England than France.

JOHN RANDOLPH (1727 or 1728–1784), unwilling to join his brother Peyton or his cousin Thomas Jefferson on the road to revolution, wrote his cousin in 1775, "We both of us seem to be steering opposite Courses." As Peyton Randolph prepared to go to Philadelphia, John Randolph was arranging to return to England along with his wife, Ariana, and their two daughters, Susannah and Ariana. He left his Virginia property in the hands of Peyton Randolph and two other trustees to be sold to pay his debts. After his death in England in 1784, Randolph's remains were brought back to Williamsburg by his daughter Ariana and her husband, James Wormeley, to be interred beside his father and brother in the chapel crypt at the College of William and Mary.

PEYTON RANDOLPH (1721?–1775) was elected president of the first Continental Congress in the fall of 1774 and of the second in May 1775. Randolph returned to Williamsburg in late May to preside over the Virginia General Assembly. (John Hancock then became president of the Continental Congress.) In Williamsburg, Randolph was greeted by local militiamen who called him "the father of your country." Later, of course, Washington would be so known. Randolph returned to Congress later that year but died suddenly in October.

SUSANNAH RANDOLPH (ca. 1755–1791), who was once rumored to be romantically linked to Lord Dunmore, left Williamsburg with her family in 1775 and lived in England, where she married John Randolph Grymes and had three children.

JAMES SOUTHALL (1726–1801 or 1802) continued to own (though not operate) the Raleigh Tavern. Though not a member of Williamsburg's elite, during and after the Revolution he gained increasing social respectability, which perhaps peaked with his appointment as a director of the Public Hospital.

JANE VOBE (dates unknown), who owned the King's Arms Tavern, may have changed its name during the Revolution. Throughout the Revolution, the tavern was a communications hub and the frequent site of important dinners and political meetings. On the eve of the siege of Yorktown, Continental officers who had accounts with Mrs. Vobe included General Thomas Nelson Jr. and Baron von Steuben. After the capital moved to Richmond in 1780, several businesses followed it.

"Mrs. Vobe's" remained in Williamsburg until 1786 when she moved her tavern to Manchester in Chesterfield County across the James River from Richmond.

GEORGE WASHINGTON (1732–1799), having won a decisive victory at Yorktown, continued to command the army, leading many to suspect he was preparing to make himself America's king. In 1783, Washington resigned his commission as commander in chief, an act that was crucial in establishing that America would have civilian rather than military rule and democracy rather than dictatorship. In 1789, he again became commander in chief, this time as part of his duties as the first president of the United States under its newly adopted Constitution. In the presidency, an office that Washington in many ways defined, he continued to profess a desire to retire, and he declined to run for a third term.

MARTHA WASHINGTON (1731–1802) accompanied her husband to Philadelphia after he became president, just as she accompanied him during the war years. After his second term, they both returned to Mount Vernon.

WILLIAM WELLS (ca. 1753–unknown), though technically not covered by Dunmore's proclamation because he was owned by a loyalist, nonetheless left Mulberry Island to join the British forces. He survived the war and later moved to Port Roseway (later renamed Port Shelburne) in Nova Scotia, a haven for many former slaves and for loyalists.

The Building of Revolutionary City

What would I have done? Which side would I have taken?

Would I have agreed that the outspoken loyalist should have been tarred and feathered for speaking out against the patriots, or "rebels" as he saw them? Would I have questioned Benedict Arnold's assessment of the "rebel" government in the spring of 1781 when I found myself paying, as Arnold said, one hundred times in taxes what I had paid before the war, before independence had been declared? As an enslaved lady's maid, would I have run to the British army and the chance of freedom, leaving behind family, friends, and a certain level of comfort even if under conditions of bondage?

In 2004, the Colonial Williamsburg Foundation's educational leaders reexamined the organization's mission to determine the best message and most meaningful experience that this renowned historic site should strive to deliver to its guests. The organization decided to rededicate itself, in a much more deliberate way, to challenging people to consider their roles and responsibilities as citizens in a self-governing society. Revolutionary City, a two-hour street theater experience, was developed as the primary vehicle to deliver this message.

Williamsburg, along with Boston and Philadelphia, is one of the most important birthplaces of American independence. Revolutionary City uses the dramas of Williamsburg's history to provoke guests to examine the legacies of the American Revolution. The goal is to challenge citizens to apply the lessons of the Revolution to current issues.

STREET THEATER

Why choose a theatrical model for this very ambitious undertaking?

Colonial Williamsburg has used character portrayal, or "first-person" interpretation, as a presentation method since 1980. Guests most often met with individual characters in parlors, kitchens, or tavern rooms and engaged in conversations centered on that particular character's life and circumstances. These slice-of-life encounters were designed to paint broad pictures of colonial life, to provide insights into the material and philosophical world of British American culture. The character interpretation program was very well received, but it was limited in its reach and in its ability to communicate broader stories and themes. While these encounters were informative, they were not designed to help guests see parallels between the colonial world in revolution and our own culture.

During the 1990s, Colonial Williamsburg experimented with reenacting some of the seminal events that occurred in Williamsburg during the Revolution, many of which are now portrayed in Revolutionary City. While these reenactments enjoyed some success, their effectiveness was hit-or-miss because they were not scripted and only minimally staged and many of the staff members portraying characters did not possess sufficient acting skills.

These programs did, however, demonstrate one undeniable truth: guests loved meeting and interacting with historical characters when they were well researched and skillfully performed. Evaluations of these programs revealed that their themes were most successfully communicated by skilled actors performing well-staged, well-constructed narratives. The lessons learned about applying theatrical disciplines to historical interpretation, coupled with the goal of provoking guests to think about citizenship, gave birth to Revolutionary City.

Getting the Show on the Road (or Street)

Teams of administrators, historians, program planners, and historical interpreters got to work. A program team identified and developed the stories. Another team coordinated, communicated, and oversaw the logistical elements of the production. A third team developed a job description and a casting process for the performers.

The program team examined the historical narrative that makes up Williamsburg's Revolutionary story. Debates ensued between historians and dramatists as to which events and incidents would constitute the most effective experience and best challenge the audience to think about citizenship then and now. The Revolution was the story, but when did it start and when did it end? And what were the turning points, the dramatic moments of no return? The essence of drama is conflict. The success of this theatrical experience would depend on identifying the essential conflicts within the Revolutionary narrative.

The event chosen to open Revolutionary City took place on May 26, 1774. Virginia's royal governor, Lord Dunmore, dissolved the House of Burgesses for protesting the closing of Boston Harbor by the British parliament as a consequence of the Boston Tea Party. The House of Burgesses had been dissolved on other occasions in the past for protesting British tax policies, but this time was different. This time the burgesses were not protesting a tax but the removal of basic civil liberties that had always been granted to British Americans. Secondly, and most critically to the story, instead of passively accepting their punishment as they often had in the past, Virginia's leaders decided to continue and heighten their protest. They called for a congress of representatives from all the colonies to meet "to protect the united interests of America." This was a turning point, a point of no return. This was drama.

The program team went on to identify the other Williamsburg stories that would inform and intensify the plot, leading to climactic moments that would define the Revolutionary experience.

The war years had never received much attention in programming and interpretation from Colonial Williamsburg. The program team determined to change that and turn a passive colonial story into a much more active Revolutionary narrative. The passage of the Virginia Declaration of Rights (the forerunner of the Bill of Rights) protecting such freedoms as speech, religion, trial by jury, and the right to bear arms; the adoption of Virginia's constitution; the first years of republican government with Patrick Henry and Thomas Jefferson serving as the first elected governors in Virginia's history; the removal of the capital from Williamsburg to Richmond in the spring of 1780, beginning Williamsburg's decline as a political, cultural, and commercial center; the brief appearance of Benedict Arnold as commander of a British occupation force in April 1781: all of these were dramatic milestones in Williamsburg's history and critical events that needed to find their way into its Revolutionary story.

With the plot outlined and the story elements defined, the decision was made to divide Revolutionary City into three "acts" that play out over the seven days of each week from mid-March to mid-November. Act I, "The Collapse of Royal Government," occurs on Tuesdays, Thursdays, and Saturdays. Through seven scripted scenes that follow the timeline from May 1774 through May 1776, it re-creates the events that motivated most free Virginians to transform themselves from subjects of the British monarch to citizens of a free and independent nation.

Act II, "Citizens at War," Wednesdays, Fridays, and Sundays, again enacted through seven formal scenes, chronicles the war years in Williamsburg from the arrival of news of the Declaration of Independence on July 26, 1776, to the departure of George Washington and the allied French and American armies from Williamsburg to Yorktown on September 28, 1781.

Act III, "Building a Nation," plays on Mondays, bookended by addresses from two of Virginia's historic giants, Patrick Henry and George Washington. This act also features the stories of preachers, house servants, husbandmen, actors, and artisans enslaved and free. These were nation builders no less than Washington and Henry.

STICKING TO THE SCRIPT

All the scenes in Revolutionary City are derived from documented events that occurred in Williamsburg. All characters have been taken from the historical record. Much of the dialogue in the scripts is based on primary documentation. Significant passages are literally lifted from the documents themselves. In some cases, the scenes represent actual events: such is the case with the opening scene of act 1 in which Lord Dunmore dissolves the House of Burgesses. In the scene, Dunmore issues the dissolution statement that was quoted in the May 26, 1774, *Virginia Gazette:* "I Have in my Hand a Paper, published by Order of your House, conceived in such Terms as reflect highly upon his Majesty and the Parliament of Great Britain; which makes it necessary for me to dissolve you, and you are dissolved accordingly."

Other examples of lines taken directly from the historical record can be found in "A Court of Tar and Feathers," the scene that represents the extemporaneous "court-martial" or trial of loyalist Joshua Hardcastle for speaking out against patriots and in favor of the British king. This event occurred on September 3, 1775. The script is based on an account of the trial that appeared in a Williamsburg newspaper the following week. When James Innes, the officer directing the court-martial, informs Hardcastle that he is accused of frequently speaking of "the cause of America in a most disgraceful and menacing manner"; when he declares that the actions he and the other soldiers are taking are motivated by thinking themselves "bound, by the ties of honour and love of country" and because they are "exasperated at this insulting behaviour"; when, at the end of the scene, he admonishes the crowd that they should all see this "as a warning to those who may hereafter sport with the great and glorious cause of America," Innes is speaking lines that are taken straight from the 1775 newspaper account.

Many scenes use the historical record as a jumping-off point for exploring the human dramas that played out in reaction to Revolutionary events. "A House Divided" enacts a confrontation between young Susannah Randolph and her mother, Ariana, the daughter and wife of the resolute loyalist John Randolph. The documentary record tells us that John Randolph left Virginia with his wife and two daughters in September 1775 in the face of growing tensions. Remaining behind was his son, Edmund, who in fact received an officer's commission and served briefly on General George Washington's staff. This scene sheds light on the torment of families divided by the American Revolution. In "A House Divided," mother confronts daughter with the decision to leave for England, and daughter confronts mother with the reality that brother Edmund will remain behind.

Two scenes in Revolutionary City portray the dilemma faced by many in the "other half" of the Williamsburg community, the enslaved African Americans who comprised more than 50 percent of the city's population. "Liberty to Slaves!" and "Running to Freedom" bring to light the traumas and choices of slaves who were offered the opportunity to gain freedom by running away from masters who had chosen to break with Great Britain. These scenes are based on two documents that were issued by British officials at different stages of the Revolution. The first document, known as Dunmore's Proclamation, was issued by our same Lord Dunmore in October 1775 at the beginning of the war. The scene "Liberty to Slaves!" reveals the heartbreak of an enslaved man named William Wells who learns that the promised freedom of the proclamation is extended only to men enslaved by "rebel" masters, or those American patriots fighting against the British. William Wells's master was a loyalist, and the proclamation therefore offered him no hope.

"Running to Freedom" is based on the story of Eve, a woman enslaved in the Elizabeth Randolph household, who ran away to follow the British army to Yorktown, at what was to be the end of the war. As many as eight hundred enslaved Virginians had taken this path, following the army of General Lord Cornwallis. Their hopes had been pinned on the Phillipsburg Proclamation issued by British General Henry Clinton from his headquarters in Phillipsburg, New York, on June 30, 1779. The Phillipsburg Proclamation had not in fact promised freedom to slaves, only employment with the army if they would come to its assistance.

All the scenes and stories invite audience members to vicariously cast themselves into the roles of members of the Williamsburg community during the American Revolution. While guests are not literally assigned roles, they are referred to by the characters in scripted scenes or in informal interactions as if they are part of the community.

At its core, Revolutionary City is about people living their lives against the backdrop of momentous world-changing events. Whether founding famous or ignoble, rich or poor, free or enslaved, man or woman, they all influenced or were influenced by visions of the American dream and by the promises of the Declaration of Independence, both realized and unfulfilled.

Actor Interpreters

In order to achieve a more theatrical approach to the experience, a new category of museum professional was created: the actor interpreter. A job description indicates that the performers must be proficient in memorizing and performing scripts and other elements of basic stagecraft. They must also be able to conduct research on historical subjects, analyze documentation, and then apply their analyses to the characters that they are to portray. Scripted scenes are the framework of the Revolutionary City experience, but actors and interpreters must also be able to convert their analyses into improvisation in the personas of their historical characters in order to informally engage guests. These improvisations must involve both the audience and other characters.

The job description states that the performer must be able to portray an eighteenth-century Virginia character. It is very important that the actors who work in Revolutionary City have a look and a presence that is representative of the time period and culture, as revealed by visual sources such as paintings and prints. Physical descriptions from written sources, including novels, plays, and diaries, contribute to the picture as well.

The audition process included three stages. Actors were required to perform a monologue from a stage or screenplay that had been written since 1900. A more contemporary piece allowed directors and producers to gauge acting skills. If the actor demonstrated proficient dramatic skills, then she or he was asked to perform some readings from period historical pieces. The period readings allowed directors to see the actor in the historical context, to see how she or he would "read" (the theatrical term) as a historical character. The actors who were successful in the audition phases were then interviewed to determine how effective they would be as team members and guest service providers, both critical skills to the potential success of Revolutionary City and the continuing quality of the Colonial Williamsburg experience.

In the first week of January 2006, the thirty-eight actors who had been hired into the Revolutionary City cast began a ten-week training and rehearsal process. Most of those hired had previous experience as Colonial Williamsburg interpreters, several from the former character interpreter group. Those who were new to Colonial Williamsburg received basic instruction in the history of Williamsburg and Virginia in the seventeenth and eighteenth centuries. Everyone had to learn and practice appropriate period customs, behavior, and deportment. Everyone also researched their characters with guidance from Colonial Williamsburg historians. The final four weeks were spent rehearsing the scripted scenes and developing improvisations related to those scenes and the overall Revolutionary City story line.

On March 20, 2006, after more than a year's preparation, Revolutionary City was launched. Revolutionary City plays daily to audiences ranging in size from five to eight hundred during the busiest times, mostly in the spring season, down to two to three hundred during the slower seasons. The success of this approach has been demonstrated by glowing reviews and by responses in guest surveys.

Bill Weldon
Director, Historic Area
Programs and Productions

Sources for Reprinted Historical Material

Throughout this book, characters and documents are sometimes quoted verbatim from historical documents and recordings of historical proceedings. Below are those quotations that were taken from the historical record along with their source material.

7: "If this be treason, make the most of it."

Patrick Henry in response to the Stamp Act as recorded by his biographer William Wirt in *Sketches of the Life and Character of Patrick Henry* (New York, 1817), 65.

18–19: "Watertown, Wednesday near 10 o'Clock, 15th April, 1775.
To all friends of American Liberty, be it known, that this morning, before break of day a brigade, consisting of about 1000 or 1200 men, landed at Phips's farm, at Cambridge, and marched to Lexington, where they found a company of our colony militia in arms, upon whom they fired without any provocation, killed 6 men, and wounded 4 others. . . ."

"New-York, Sunday 23d April, 1775. The following interesting advices, were this day received here, by two vessels from Newport, and by an express by land." An American Time Capsule: Three Centuries of Broadsides and Other Printed Ephemera, Printed Ephemera collection, Rare Book and Special Collections Division, Library of Congress, portfolio 108, folder 5.

21: "Your dependence on l - - d D - - - - e has indeed promoted your own disgrace."

Pinkney's *Virginia Gazette* (Williamsburg), July 27, 1775, page 3.

29: "all indented servants, negroes, or others (appertaining to rebels) free, that are able and willing to bear arms"

Pinkney's *Virginia Gazette* (Williamsburg), November, 23, 1775, page 2.

30: "And I do hereby farther declare all indented servants, negroes, or others (appertaining to rebels) free, that are able and willing to bear arms."

Pinkney's *Virginia Gazette* (Williamsburg), November, 23, 1775, page 2.

37: "to concur with the Delegates of the other Colonies in declaring Independency"

Peter Force, ed., *American Archives: Containing a Documentary History of the English Colonies in North America, from the King's Message to Parliament, of March 7, 1774, to the Declaration of Independence, by the United States,* 4th ser., vol. 5 (Washington, 1844), 860.

37–39: The Preamble and Resolutions of the Virginia Convention, adopted May 15, 1776, as reprinted in Brent Tarter, ed., *Revolutionary Virginia: The Road to Independence,* vol. 7, part 1, *Independence and the Fifth Convention, 1776: A Documentary Record* (Charlottesville, VA: University Press of Virginia, 1983), 142–143.

40: "prepare a Declaration of Rights and such a plan of government as will be most likely to maintain peace and order in this colony and secure substantial and equal liberty to the people"

From the Preamble and Resolutions of the Virginia Convention, adopted May 15, 1776, as reprinted in Tartar, *Revolutionary Virginia,* vol. 7, part 1, 143.

40: "in all the revolutions of time, of human opinion, and of government, a perpetual standard should be erected, around which the people might rally and . . . be forever admonished to be watchful, firm, and virtuous"

Edmund Randolph, *History of Virginia,* ed. Arthur H. Shaffer (Charlottesville, VA: University Press of Virginia, 1970), 255.

40: "All Men are by nature equally free and Independent and have certain inherent Rights . . . namely the enjoyment of Life and liberty . . . and pursuing and obtaining happiness."

From the Virginia Declaration of Rights, adopted June 12, 1776, as reprinted in Tartar, *Revolutionary Virginia,* vol. 7, part 2, 449.

40: "that all men are created equal," "certain unalienable Rights, that among these are Life, Liberty and the pursuit of Happiness"

From the Declaration of Independence, adopted July 4, 1776, as reprinted by the U. S. National Archives and Records Administration, www.archives.gov, February 17, 2009.

41–42: Virginia Declaration of Rights, adopted June 12, 1776, as reprinted in Tartar, *Revolutionary Virginia,* vol. 7, part 2, 449–450.

45: "That these United Colonies are, and of right ought to be, free and independent States"

Journals of the Continental Congress, 1774–1789, vol. 5, June 5–October 8, 1776 (Washington, DC: Government Printing Office, 1905), 425.

45: "at the head of each brigade of the continental army posted at and near New York," "every where received with loud huzzas and the utmost demonstrations of joy," "the just desert [sic] of an ungrateful tyrant"

Purdie's *Virginia Gazette* (Williamsburg), July 26, 1776, page 2.

46: "be solemnly proclaimed at four oClock in the afternoon on Thursday next at the Capitol in the City of Williamsburg also at the Court of Hustings, and at the Palace; that the Mayor of the said City be made acquainted therewith, and requested with the Corporation to give their attendance.
"Also that the Commanding Officer of the Continental Forces be informed thereof and desired to give orders for the Army to parade on that occasion."

H. R. McIlwaine, *Journals of the Council of the State of Virginia*, vol. 1 (Richmond, VA: 1931), 83.

46: "amidst the acclamations of the people"

Purdie's *Virginia Gazette* (Williamsburg), July 26, 1776, page 2.

47–50: Declaration of Independence, adopted July 4, 1776, as reprinted by the U.S. National Archives and Records Administration, www.archives.gov, February 17, 2009.

57: "an Act of equal Inhumanity and Injustice to the Indians, that cannot fail to be attended with fatal Consequences"

Collections of the Massachusetts Historical Society, 4th ser., vol. 10 (Boston: 1871), 726.

57: "a considerable Mob gather'd about us"

"Report by Lieutenant-Governor Henry Hamilton on His Proceedings from November, 1776 to June, 1781," as quoted in James Alton James, ed., *George Rogers Clark Papers, 1771–1781*, Collections of the Illinois State Historical Library, vol. 8, Virginia Series, vol. 3 (Springfield, IL.: 1912), 197.

63: "We have the honor of enclosing you a copy of a letter . . . which was handed [to] us immediately on our being put on board this ship. . . . We . . . beg leave to observe, that should it fall to the lot of all, or any of us, to be made victims, . . . we have only to regret that our blood cannot be disposed of more to the advancement of the glorious cause to which we have adhered. A separate roll of our names attend this letter.

"With the greatest respect, we are, sir,

"Your most obedient and humble servants,

STEPHEN MOORE, Lieut. Col. N[orth] Carolina Militia.

JOHN BARNWELL, Major So[uth] Carolina Militia,

for ourselves and 130 prisoners."

R. W. Gibbes, *Documentary History of the American Revolution, Consisting of Letters and Papers Relating to the Contest for Liberty, Chiefly in South Carolina, in 1781 and 1782, from Originals in the Possession of the Editor and from Other Sources* (Columbia, SC: 1853), 74–75.

65: "ungrateful returns I have received from my countrymen"

The Writings of George Washington; Being His Correspondence, Addresses, Messages, and Other Papers, Official and Private, Selected and Published from the Original Manuscripts . . . vol. 6, ed. Jared Sparks (Boston: 1834), 523.

73: "And Moses went and spake these words unto all Israel. . . .

"The Lord thy God, he will go over before thee, and he will destroy these nations from before thee, and thou shalt possess them. . . .

"And the Lord shall give them up before your face, that ye may do unto them according unto all the commandments which I have commanded you.

"Be strong and of a good courage, fear not, nor be afraid of them: for the Lord thy God, he it is that doth go with thee; he will not fail thee, nor forsake thee."

Deuteronomy 31:1–6 (King James Version).

75: "Be strong and of a good courage, fear not, nor be afraid of them . . ."

". . . for the Lord thy God, he it is that doth go with thee."

Deut. 31:6.

77: "The boy cannot escape me."

General Charles Cornwallis in a letter that was intercepted, according to the marquis de Lafayette, *Memoirs, Correspondence and Manuscripts of General Lafayette,* vol. 1 (New York: 1837), 263–267, as reprinted in Henry Steele Commager and Richard B. Morris, eds., *The Spirit of 'Seventy-Six: The Story of the American Revolution as Told by Participants* (New York: Harper & Row, 1975), 1207.

77: "Every day we loose [sic] now, is comparatively an age. . . . Hurry on then . . . with your Troops upon the wing of Speed."

George Washington to Benjamin Lincoln, 15 September 1781, in *The Writings of George*

Washington from the Original Manuscript Sources, 1745–1799, vol. 23, ed. John C. Fitzpatrick (Washington, DC: 1937), 119.

77: "I hope you will keep Lord Cornwallis safe, without Provisions or Forage untill we arrive."

George Washington to the marquis de Lafayette, 10 September 1781, in Fitzpatrick, *Writings of George Washington*, 110.

77: "with an ardor not easily described"

St. George Tucker to Mrs. Tucker, 15 September 1781, Tucker-Coleman Papers, Swem Library, College of William and Mary, Williamsburg, Virginia. (CWF microfilm 1021.3)

80: "gone to the enemy"

This notation in Betty Randolph's handwriting appears on an inventory of Peyton Randolph's property held by the Library of Congress. (CWF microfilm 1005)

80: "Eve's bad behaviour laid me under the necessity of selling her."

Betty Randolph's will, York County, Va., Wills and Inventories, No. 23, 1783–1811, pp. 4–5. (CWF microfilm 1.12)

80: "promise that he never would be guilty of a like offence," "as a warning to those who may hereafter sport with the great and glorious cause of America"

Pinkney's *Virginia Gazette* (Williamsburg), September 7, 1775, page 3.

80: "to leave this Continent within ten Days"

Dixon and Hunter's *Virginia Gazette* (Williamsburg), November 1, 1776, page 4.

80: "to leave the Country immediately"

Dixon and Hunter's *Virginia Gazette* (Williamsburg), May 9, 1777, page 4.

80: "If this be treason, make the most of it."

Patrick Henry in May 1765 to the Virginia House of Burgesses in response to the Stamp Act as recorded by his biographer William Wirt in *Sketches*, 65.

80: "Give me liberty, or give me death."

Patrick Henry in March 1775 at the second Virginia Convention putting forward a resolution that the colony immediately be put in a state of defense as recorded by Wirt in *Sketches*, 123.

80: "for grand impressions in the defense of liberty, the Western world has not yet been able to exhibit a rival"

Randolph, *History of Virginia*, 181.

81: "Barbara the wife of Alexander Hoy a poor Soldier in the Service of the Commonwealth is allowed twelve pounds towards the support of herself and Children she being unable to provide for them."

York County, Va., Records, Order Book 4 (1774–1784), December 15, 1777, p. 153. (CWF microfilm 1.33)

81: "wife of a Soldier in the service of the Continent"

York County, Va., Records, Order Book 4 (1774–1784), June 21, 1779, p. 218. (CWF microfilm 1.33)

81: "splendid, magnificent and sufficient to shake the human mind"

Patrick Henry during a debate on the ratification of the Constitution in the Virginia Convention on June 25, 1788, as reprinted in John P. Kaminski and Gaspare J. Saladino, *The Documentary History of the Ratification of the Constitution*, vol. 10, *Ratification of the Constitution by the States: Virginia*, 3 (Madison: State Historical Society of Wisconsin, 1993), 1536.

82: "a man of the first order of wisdom among those who acted on the theatre of the revolution, of expansive mind, profound judgment, cogent in argument, learned in the lore of our former constitution, and earnest for the republican change on democratic principles"

The Works of Thomas Jefferson, vol. 1, ed. Paul Leicester Ford (New York: G. P. Putnam's Sons, 1904), 65.

82: "benevolent and liberal," "haughty and austere"

Randolph, *History of Virginia*, 185.

82: "to declare the United Colonies free and independent states"

From Resolutions of the Virginia Convention Calling upon Congress for a Declaration of Independence as reprinted in *The Letters and Papers of Edmund Pendleton, 1734–1803*, vol. 1, ed. David John Mays (Charlottesville: University Press of Virginia, 1967), 178–179.

83: "For Gods Sake return to your Family & indeed to yourself."

John Randolph to Edmund Randolph, 12 August 1775, Gage Papers, William L. Clements Library, University of Michigan. (CWF microfilm 1031)

83: "increasing rancor," "an impossibility"

Edmund Randolph to his children, 23 March 1810, MS #4263, Alderman Library, University of Virginia, Charlottesville.

83: "We both of us seem to be steering opposite Courses."

The Papers of Thomas Jefferson, vol. 1, 1760–1776, ed. Julian P. Boyd (Princeton, NJ: Princeton University Press, 1950), 244.

83: "the father of your country"

Pinkney's *Virginia Gazette* (Williamsburg), June 1, 1775, page 3.

87: "I Have in my Hand a Paper, published by Order of your House, conceived in such Terms as reflect highly upon his Majesty and the Parliament of Great Britain; which makes it necessary for me to dissolve you, and you are dissolved accordingly."

Purdie and Dixon's *Virginia Gazette* (Williamsburg), May 26, 1774, page 2.

87: "the cause of America in a most disgraceful and menacing manner," "bound, by the ties of honour and love of country," "exasperated at this insulting behaviour," "as a warning to those who may hereafter sport with the great and glorious cause of America"

Dixon and Hunter's *Virginia Gazette* (Williamsburg), September 9, 1775, page 3.